AUSTRALIA'S AGE OF IRON:

HISTORY AND ARCHAEOLOGY

AUSTRALIA'S AGE OF IRON:

HISTORY AND ARCHAEOLOGY

R. Ian Jack and Aedeen Cremin

OXFORD UNIVERSITY PRESS
SYDNEY UNIVERSITY PRESS

OXFORD UNIVERSITY PRESS
in association with
SYDNEY UNIVERSITY PRESS

National Library of Australia
Cataloguing-in-Publication data:

Jack, R. Ian (Robert Ian), 1935- .
Australia's age of iron

Bibliography
Includes index.
ISBN 0 424 00158 6.

1. Iron industry and trade - Australia - History.
2. Industrial archaeology - Australia.
I. Cremin, Aedeen, 1940- . II. Title.

338.476691410994

Cover photograph by R. Ian Jack
Design Sarn Potter Graphics
Printed by Kyodo Printing Company, Singapore
Published by Sydney University Press in association
with Oxford University Press,
253 Normanby Road, South Melbourne, Australia

Dedicated to the memory of Maureen Byrne (1953–1977),
whose archaeological work at Lithgow and Mittagong
was an inspiration for this book.

CONTENTS

ACKNOWLEDGEMENTS

This book grew out of a wide involvement in the industrial archaeology of New South Wales, in which the mining and processing of minerals is a recurrent theme. Teaching programmes at the University of Sydney, the pioneer of academic historical archaeology in Australia, coupled with an increasing participation in heritage activities, brought the two authors together in a study of the Lithgow Valley over a decade ago. Later collaboration in a Southern Highlands heritage study placed Fitzroy Ironworks centre stage and thereafter it was obviously necessary to research the experience of other states in the nineteenth century.

Ian Jack was responsible for all the site visits in Tasmania, South Australia and Victoria. In Tasmania explorations of the Tamar Valley sites of blast-furnaces, iron-mines, processing areas and communications could not have been achieved without the help of those vigorous in running the Grubb Shaft Museum at Beaconsfield, particularly Dick Hooper but also Kevin Joyce and Danny O'Reilly. The owners of Ilfracombe, Craig and Cheryl Sheehan, were founts of help, local knowledge and goodwill. For access to Swift's Jetty, we are grateful to the owner, Jerry Baxter. Mrs Jill Willey was generous in correcting misapprehensions about the manager's house at Redbill Point. At Launceston, the staff at the Queen Victoria Museum and Art Gallery, both at its main building and at its Local History photographic collection, and Judith Hollingsworth, the Local Studies librarian at the Launceston branch of the State Library, were constructive and courteous.

The technical expertise of Don Reynolds, from Wollongong, and Hugh Wellington, from Launceston, was most freely shared in talk and letters about the interpretation of Ilfracombe, and the final clarification of most of the uncertainties surrounding this key site was made possible by the newspaper research undertaken for us in Hobart by Kristen Erskine.

In South Australia, Ian Jack's visit to Mount Jagged was made simpler by the advance reconnoitre by Peter Bell and Patrick Martin, who also came to the site and shared in the mud-bath.

Iain Stuart from what was then the Victoria Archaeological Survey drove Ian Jack to Lal Lal and explored the blast-furnace site in a traditional Ballarat downpour, with the consolation prize of adding a major brickworks to his collection.

In New South Wales much assistance has been given in previous years for our various studies of Lithgow. Our 1986 study of the blast-furnace site was carried out in association with J. N. L. Southern and John Gibson, and with considerable help from Don Reynolds and Jerry Platt, all of whom it is a pleasure to thank again. The site was surveyed then by Chris Padgen, with some detailed work by postgraduate Historical Archaeology students from the University of Sydney.

The generosity of Brian Rogers, of the University of Wollongong, in loaning the rediscovered Fitzroy minute-book for 1864 to 1872 made the heart of our Mittagong chapter far more exhaustive and original than we had dared to hope. The assignment done by Patricia Thams on the Fitzroy site as part of her university coursework in 1991 was the basis for our plan of the foundations. For comments on the company town in Mittagong, we are grateful to Penny Pike, Jocelyn Colleran and members of ICOMOS. For access to the archives and photographs of the Berrima and District Historical Society, we thank John Simons and Geoffrey Squires.

We are most grateful to Professor Emeritus Max Hatherly for casting his metallurgist's eye over the text and saving us from some scientific infelicities.

Colleagues, librarians and curators have been generous in telling us of relevant illustrations in out-of-the-way places: in particular we thank Linda Young, Leigh McCawley and Alan Davies.

For the production of maps and site-plans we are grateful to John Roberts and Peter Johnson in the Cartography section of the University of Sydney's Department of Geography.

The chapters based on fieldwork outside New South Wales have been written by Ian Jack, those on Lithgow by both authors and the Fitzroy and Bogolong chapters are based on Ian Jack's archival work and Aedeen Cremin's archaeological surveys.

LIST OF ILLUSTRATIONS

Feeding Diderot's furnace. The man at G is about to empty a basket into the furnace mouth, which is cut away by the artist. The water-wheel powers the two bellows under the skillion roof marked H to supply a cold blast to the adjacent furnace. (D. Diderot, *Recueil des Planches*, 3me livraison vol. 4, Paris 1765, Forges, section 2, plate 7)

THE AGE OF IRON

A blast furnace is really a stomach which needs feeding regularly, consistently and continuously. Lack of food upsets it, but too much or the wrong sort makes it sicken, belch and demand quick relief.[1]

To the eighteenth-century *Encyclopédistes* the processing of iron ranked with the consumption of food as a universal basic of civilized life. The vividness of the imagery, moreover, puts the ironmaster firmly on the threshold of shame. The century of the *Encyclopédie* was a final stage in suppressing that free talk about bodily functions which had been so striking a part of life, at every social level, in the Middle Ages and early modern Europe. What had been commonplace to Chaucer became, over a century and a half, an object of Erasmus' ironic strictures, and by the time of Diderot was a shameful act.[2] The ironmaster who fed his furnace unwisely stood on the cusp of shame. He must neither starve it nor over-indulge it, and his function is a key one of industrial responsibility.

The ironmaster had inherited the status of the smith, who had powers as much supernatural as practical. At the very heart of Wagner's *Ring* are those who work metal, either the gold of the Rhinemaidens and the Nibelung, or the magic iron sword, Nothung. Who can recombine the broken fragments of Nothung? Only 'he who knows no fear', the hero Siegfried. In traditional productions of *Siegfried*, the hero melts the sword-pieces in a crucible while his left hand works a blacksmith's bellows to fan the fire, the simple, effective way of heating iron used for more than two thousand years before the historic Siegfried and still used by craft smiths all over the world. In the centenary production of the *Ring* at Bayreuth, the forging of Nothung became a scene from the Industrial Revolution in which a huge drop-hammer replaced the simple anvil beside a hearth. The power of the image and the power of the opéra remained, but something of the supernatural ability of a mere mortal to conquer iron had been transferred to the great machine, itself cast from iron.

So it is with the blast-furnace, created by centuries and millennia of experiment and audacity to perform a primordial miracle, the creation of iron fit for the blacksmith's forge, from the complex ores found in every continent and virtually every country. This blast-furnace, swallowing the ironstone and, through the application of the right fuel and the right flux at the right temperature, separating it into usable iron on the one hand and slag on the other, was the prerequisite for the smith's magic. Wayland the Smith and Sandford the Lithgow ironmaster belong to the same masculine world, linked by their power over the metal that for more than three thousand years has been critically important. Even today, with a plethora of synthetics, iron is fundamental. It can do things that bronze or wood or plastics cannot do. Tools of stone or bone or wood or other metals existed before iron tools and coexisted with them, but iron could uniquely be produced in massive quantities and could be reworked in the glowing hearth to remain sharp and true. Iron tools can be sharpened and resharpened: the knife for aggression or domesticity and the axe which felled the forests and created both agriculture and desert could become ubiquitous only when made of iron.

Iron 'is equally serviceable to the arts, the sciences, to agriculture, and war; the same ore furnishes the sword, the ploughshare, the scythe, the pruning hook, the needle, the graver, the spring of a watch or of a carriage, the chisel, the chain, the anchor, the compass, the cannon, and the bomb. It is a medicine of much virtue, and the only metal friendly to the human frame'. Andrew Ure, that normally dour Scotsman, went on to rhapsodize: 'iron accommodates itself to all our wants, our desires, and even our caprices.'[3]

Without iron being smelted in increasingly large quantities, the Industrial Revolution of the eighteenth and nineteenth centuries would have been impossible. And however fine the foundries to work wrought-iron and to pour remelted pig-iron into increasingly elaborate casting moulds, the primary need in 1800, as in 1500 or 1200, was to maintain the supply of new raw iron smelted from that most common but most chemically diverse of ores, ironstone in all its myriad forms.

Ironstone is almost always a compound. Metallic iron is found in the remains of meteors which have struck the earth; some metallic iron has been spewed to the surface by the Greenland volcanoes; very occasionally outcrops of ironstone contain knobs of relatively pure iron. All of these natural fragments of metallic iron can be, and have been, hammered into small tools or ornaments by cultures as separate as the Inuit and the pre-dynastic peoples of Egypt. Even in South Australia surface iron was 'found so pure that it has, without any preparation, been welded on to a piece of manufactured iron'.[4] But the prodigious quantities of iron compounds found near the surface of the earth are the only possible source for a successful Iron Age. And the Iron

Age of prehistory, of the Romans, of later Europe, America, Asia and Africa, gives way to the Age of Iron only in the Industrial Revolution—which was made possible by iron but also created the final hegemony of iron.

It has always been a challenge to extract usable iron in sufficient quantity and at an affordable cost from ferrous and ferric compounds. Iron ore not only consists of different iron oxides but characteristically contains small proportions of other metals, such as tungsten, titanium, copper or chromium; it also contains salts other than oxides, such as iron sulphides, sulphates or chlorides. Some of these differences seemed visible to the eye, so that there are basic ore types called red hematite (a ferric oxide without much water content), and others called brown hematite (a ferric oxide with water present), but even at this most elementary level the colour of the ore is not a regular red or brown; some 'brown hematite' is red, some yellow. Other substances are, moreover, often combined with the hematite, such as sulphur, manganese or silica. Within quite a small area of iron deposits there can be much variety in these trace elements, which can change the chemistry of the smelted iron quite dramatically: the luckless British and Tasmanian Charcoal Iron Company found to its cost that the chromium content in its ironstone deposits created difficulties which were not shared by the two other iron companies nearby in the Tamar Valley.

The challenge to the smelting industry, even after detailed analysis of ores became commonplace in the nineteenth century, did not disappear and is present today. The simultaneous challenge to combine the iron within the blast-furnace with useful elements, especially carbon, was similarly learnt by trial and error and later refined by science.

These challenges have been omnipresent and, when successfully resolved, enhanced the supernatural qualities of the ironworkers in the popular mind. The stages in developing technologies to meet these challenges are not, however, to be seen as a straight line of progress. 'It is doubtful that we will ever return to the concept that, because the physical properties of metals remain constant regardless of the historical or cultural setting in which they were being used, metallurgical discovery must follow an inevitable sequence.'[5] The iron of the Hittites in the second millennium BC, the dominance of the European Celts over iron as well as salt in the first millennium BC, the extraordinarily developed hot blast-furnaces of the Han dynasty in China in the four hundred years around the birth of Christ, the experiments with steel-making in India and the Arab world of the first millennium AD, and the progressive creation and improvement of the European blast-furnace proper over the last six hundred years are not orderly steps on an inevitable path. They are not the product of systematic diffusion; many successes arose from individual experimentation in widely separated parts of the world; and the chronological sequence is not one of simple technological progression.

This book is concerned primarily with one aspect of the winning of

Catalan forge. (A. Ure, *Dictionary of Arts, Manufactures and Mines*, 5th edn, 1860, p. 945, fig. 1218)

usable iron, the process of smelting ore in Australia. There are two broad divisions of historical smelting, which have coexisted in different societies at particular periods. The first is the reduction of ore by heating lumps of iron ore in an oven to produce not molten iron but a spongy mass, a 'bloom', from which remaining impurities were partly removed by hammering. The characteristic fuel used to reduce ore to a bloom was charcoal and the high temperature needed was created either by natural wind-draughts or by some form of bellows.

There were many versions of this basic form, conveniently known as the Catalan forge, which is the Mediterranean version developed in the fifteenth century and still in operation until very modern times.

The bloomery, whether Catalan or not, is simply a development of a blacksmith's forge. Basically it consists of a hearth, usually with a stone or fire-brick base, covered with a pile of charcoal as fuel. The lumps of iron ore are placed on top and in front of the charcoal and the heap is usually coated with a mixture of ground-up ore and charcoal dust moistened to create a semi-seal. Air is introduced under pressure from the back, on to the charcoal, either by natural wind or by bellows forcing air through a narrow tube called a tuyere. The iron oxide called brown hematite, limonite or bog iron, which contains a good deal of water, was the most suitable form of ore for such a furnace. In the mid-nineteenth century the Catalan forges in the Mediterranean area usually held at most 0.5 tonne of ore. 'Those formerly in use in Austria, and to some extent still in America (*e.g.*, the Champlain forge), have the blast heated to a greater or lesser extent by the waste flames from the forge.'[6] The style of this furnace evolved independently in many parts of the world: in India, Africa, Borneo and Madagascar as well as Europe. It was taken by Europeans to the new lands of the Americas and ultimately to Australia. The rich diversity of such furnaces in Africa, owing nothing to outside influence or to the example of ceramic kilns, is remarkable and instructive.

> The African furnaces differ among themselves not only in form but also in the technique used. Furthermore, smelters located in close geographical and temporal proximity often have furnaces and traditions that are different. The furnace types range from open pit furnaces to highly stylized female symbols complete with legs and breasts. There are forced draft furnaces of remarkable technical sophistication capable of attaining temperatures of 1700 degrees C and tall natural draft furnaces up to 7 metres high that should be capable of a high level of production. At the other extreme there are complicated small furnaces, such as those of the Phoka, which require an extraordinary expenditure of resources for a low output of iron. These may well serve more spiritual and ritual functions than the economic production of iron.[7]

The African experience of motives beyond the economic has its parallels in other cultures and a recurrent theme of this book is the pathological optimism of those who attempted to smelt Australian ores. No blast-furnace in Australia was modelled in a female shape, but the sturdy phallicism of the Australian smelters and the invincible masculinity of the ironmasters is not too distant a counterpart.

Most of the colonial smelters, however, belong not to the class of Catalan forge but to the second broad classification, the blast-furnace proper, in which iron ore was treated in such a way that molten iron could be tapped directly from the furnace. There were many variants in the details, but the general appearance of a nineteenth-century furnace which reduced ore to molten iron was that of an upturned bottle. The blast of air, cold or, more efficiently, hot, entered near the base and the furnace was loaded with ore, fuel and flux from the top. The furnace was lined with fire-bricks to withstand the intense heat and enclosed in protective sheathing either of stone or iron.

The number of blast-furnaces at work in Britain in the mid-nineteenth century varied between 500 and 700. These furnaces actually in blast were only about half of the total number: Britain in 1878 had 948 blast-furnaces, of which only 498 were in operation. Britain led the world in number of furnaces, both in blast and idle, in the 1870s and produced more than two and a half times as much pig-iron as her nearest rival, the United States of America. The other principal players were France and Germany with, respectively, 270 and 297 furnaces in blast, 464 and 463 *in toto*, producing 1.2 million and 1.8 million tonnes of pig-iron. Belgium, for all the fame of Seraing, and its intensive secondary industry, had only 26 furnaces at work

British iron production 1860–78[9]

Year	Furnace in blast	Pig-iron production (in thousands of tonnes)
1860	582	3827
1866	618	4564
1868	560	4970
1870	664	5962
1872	702	6742
1874	649	5991
1875	629	6365
1876	585	6506
1877	541	6609
1878	498	6381

out of 61 in 1877. Sweden, which had had a significant iron industry since prehistory, had almost as many furnaces in blast as France (224 out of 325) but they were small and produced only 0.35 million tonnes in 1876, only 30 per cent of France's output. The other major producer was Austria, where 166 furnaces out of a total of 279 smelted 0.4 million tonnes of pig-iron in 1876. Britain produced virtually as much pig-iron in the 1870s as the rest of Europe and America put together[8].No other country mattered in this phase of iron production, and this is the essential context for the Australian iron industry. Whereas India and Africa had had their own pre-colonial furnaces and whereas North America had started its industry under European guidance in the seventeenth century, Australia had no experience at all of iron-making until European settlement was already three generations old in the 1840s.

But the European and American practice of iron-making in the nineteenth century was far from homogeneous, and different stages of technology overlapped as they had over millennia past.

The choice of fuel to smelt ores of different chemical combinations was a recurrent issue and there was no clear-cut answer. Although most early furnaces used charcoal and most late nineteenth-century furnaces used coke, the use of charcoal or uncoked coal remained a perfectly valid option. It is striking that in America 9 out of the 44 new blast-furnaces constructed in 1880 were intended to use charcoal.[10]

Coke had first been used successfully in England as early as 1709 by Abraham Darby at Coalbrookdale; but no French furnace used coke until 1782 and few changed from charcoal until the mid-nineteenth century.[11] The data recently published for the Western Highland Rim of Tennessee in the United States show vividly how long charcoal remained an alternative to Darby's coke. In 1876 all eleven Tennessee blast-furnaces used charcoal exclusively. In 1894 there were ten furnaces on the Western Highland Rim (including only two of those in operation 18 years earlier): eight of the ten used charcoal and only two of the eight new furnaces used coke. But in 1907 all but one of the eight blast-furnaces in the area used coke: the only charcoal iron was produced from an old furnace at Bear Spring which had been operating in the 1870s and was reopened in the late 1890s.[12]

In Pennsylvania, also, the heartland of the American iron industry, many furnaces continued to use charcoal. Hopewell Furnace, now a National Historic Site, was opened in 1772 using charcoal and it closed 111 years later, still using charcoal. A newfangled furnace burning anthracite had been built nearby in 1853 to supersede the old charcoal furnace, but it failed by 1857 and the earlier practices prevailed as long as the company survived.[13]

Both Hopewell and Tennessee are telling instances of the persistence of cold blast long into an age when pre-heated air had been demonstrated to be economical in fuel and successful in operation. At Hopewell cold blast was used throughout the long life of the charcoal furnace (although hot blast was employed for the anthracite in 1853–7). Hot blast had been patented in Britain in 1828 by the Scottish engineer James Neilson. 'Led by the inefficiency of a particular engine to his discovery that the substitution of a hot blast, instead of a refrigerated one, produced three times as much iron with the same amount of fuel', Neilson tested his idea at the Clyde Ironworks in Lanarkshire. Others challenged his patent, but the Neilson patent remained firm while it was increasingly used under licence.[14]

It is therefore interesting to see how slowly the hot blast device was introduced into Tennessee. In the 1850s out of 40 blast-furnaces on the Western Highland Rim only 5 used hot blast. By 1876 4 out of 11 were still using cold blast; only in 1893 were all the furnaces employing Neilson's innovation of 70 years before. But when the Bear Spring charcoal-fired furnace, built in 1873, reopened in 1894, it did not go over to hot blast, not even when it was burnt out and rebuilt in 1903. To the end, in the 1920s, Bear Spring persevered as a cold blast charcoal furnace on a square stone base.[15]

The experience of Tennessee is much more relevant to the Australian experience than the greater centres of European or American iron-making. The transition from charcoal to coke, which made possible the construction of much higher furnaces, was complete in South Wales by the end of the eighteenth century.[16] The impressive furnaces built at Neath Abbey in South Wales in the 1790s used coke from the outset and were of a height (17 metres and 21 metres respectively)[17] which was still rare 50 years later. Andrew Ure in 1853 commented that 'the height of the blast furnaces is very variable; some being only 36 feet [11 metres] high including the chimney, while others have an elevation of 60 feet [19 metres]. These extreme limits are very rare: so that the greater part of the furnaces are from 45 to 50 feet [14 to 16 metres] high'.[18]

Throughout the history of iron-smelting in the West in the eighteenth and nineteenth centuries, the formative period for the modern industry, there is a very great variety in technology, in raw materials and in degree of capitalization. It is, for example, instructive to compare two of the great iron centres of Glamorganshire in South Wales: Plymouth and Dowlais. The Plymouth blast-furnace near Merthyr Tydfil, established in the 1750s, used water-power for its cold blast and charcoal for fuel: it converted to coke-fuel before the end of the eighteenth century, built two more furnaces in 1800 and a fourth in 1815, but continued to use only water-power until the 1820s. The new extension of the Plymouth works at Dyffryn in 1819 and 1824 had three furnaces and there too only water-power was used. The ironmaster Anthony Hill, a man keenly interested in the chemistry and technology of his industry, who patented many innovations, and whose fourth furnace at Dyffryn was the largest in the world, to the end of his life in 1862 was operating a double water-wheel to power the blast for one of the great iron complexes in Europe.[19]

At Dowlais nearby, an even greater ironworks evolved, burning coke from the outset in 1759. It began with water-powered bellows to create the cold blast; experiments with a newly patented cylinder blower met with indifferent success, and the managers converted to a Boulton and Watt steam-engine in 1799 and installed an effective new cylinder blower in 1803.[20] By 1815 there were five furnaces at Dowlais, in 1817 two more; three new furnaces were built in 1821–3 and in the early Victorian period Dowlais expanded

Dowlais in 1840, showing the massive masonry furnaces in the background, characteristic of the late eighteenth and early nineteenth century. (Watercolour by G. Childs; original in National Library of Wales)

prodigiously with eighteen large furnaces belching fire and fumes in Childs' famous watercolours of 1840.[21] In the 1840s Dowlais was the biggest iron-smelting complex in the world with 10 000 men in its employment; yet adjoining this great works, not emulated in the Australian iron scene until Port Kembla and Newcastle fully developed in the mid-twentieth century, was Penydarren on Dowlais Brook, 'a pretty little Iron-Works, complete in every respect'.[22]

All round Britain, continental Europe and America there are examples of the coexistence of smelting technologies, of conservatism alongside experimentation, of individual responses to local circumstances and market forces. There was, of course, a broad progression. Water-power, ubiquitous in the eighteenth century, gave way to steam by the mid-nineteenth century. Charcoal fuel, universal in the seventeenth century, was very slowly edged out by coke in the eighteenth and more rapidly in the nineteenth century. Furnaces became in general much higher between 1800 and 1900, largely because coke had a crushing strength much greater than charcoal. Furnace tops which were characteristically open in the earlier nineteenth century, allowing the free escape of gases, were increasingly closed after 1850 with the efficient recycling of the furnace gases to provide heat for the blast. Cold blast was not immediately replaced by hot blast, first patented in 1828, but was adopted universally half a century after Neilson's patent expired in 1843. The stone-clad square tower of the eighteenth-century blast-furnace became less common, a circular body clad in stone and embraced by iron bands upon a square stone base became widespread in the earlier nineteenth cenury, and the fully ironclad, high furnace supported not on stone bases with arched recesses but on iron columns embedded in a strong foundation, gradually became the norm in the latter part of the nineteenth century.

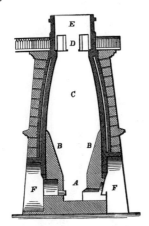 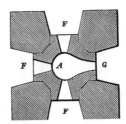

Plan and section of one of the older Dowlais furnaces. A is the hearth, B the bosh, C the upper furnace, D the charging mouth, E the tunnel head (to release the hot gases). In the section, F shows the recessed arches for the tuyeres and G the tap hole area for releasing molten iron and slag. (*Encyclopaedia Britannica*, 9th edn, 1880, XIII, p. 299, fig. 9)

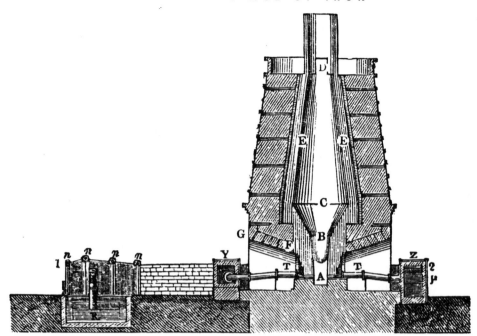

The circular, stone-faced furnace, as used in Staffordshire. A is the hearth, with air supplied through the tuyeres T; B to C is the bosh, the round base of the furnace interior, with its widest point at C (around four metres diameter). The upper furnace is lined with fire-bricks E, and tapers to the charging mouth D with the tunnel head above. (Ure, *Dictionary*, 4th edn, 1853, p. 1070, fig. 794)

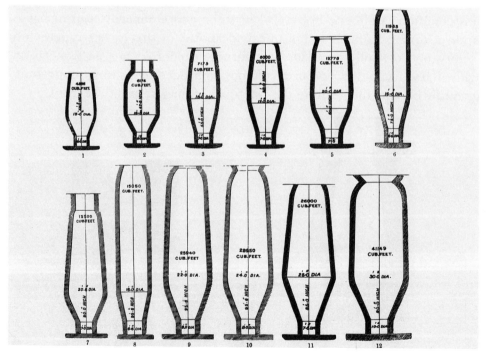

The variety of blast-furnace dimensions in the Cleveland district of Yorkshire (including Middlesbrough) between 1850 and 1870. (*Encyclopaedia Britannica*, 9th edn, 1880, XIII, p. 298, fig. 8)

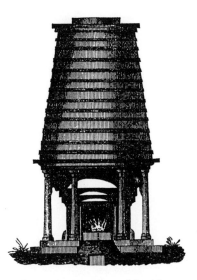

An early example of cast-iron supports for a blast-furnace, retaining an upper furnace clad in stone and bound by wrought-iron hoops, at Hyanges in France around 1850. (F. Overman, *The Manufacture of Iron in all its Various Branches*, 3rd edn, 1854, p. 178, fig. 63)

Within every one of these general progressions there were many variations and anomalies. Individual ironmasters such as Anthony Hill at Merthyr Tydfil or Sir Josiah Guest and G. T. Clark at Dowlais brought distinctive prejudices, preferences and knowledge to bear on the development of their major plants; countless lesser entrepreneurs and their managers made their own decisions, based on available capital, technological knowledge, the type of iron ore available and the range of customers expected. It should not, therefore, be a matter of surprise that the small-scale operations in the Australian colonies should have many individualistic features and that all blast-furnaces constructed during the nineteenth century in Australia combined elements of the experimental with the old-fashioned. The Australian ironmasters were not anachronistic: as in remoter American states like Tennessee, the modest size of the markets put constraints upon investment. The transition from Fitzroy's Catalan forge at Mittagong in 1848, through the vitality of the stone and iron furnaces of the 1870s, to the final success of a fully 'modern' blast-furnace at Sandford's Lithgow ironworks in 1907 is no more a simple upward curve than the American experience on the Western Highland Rim or the world-wide experience of the nineteenth century.

Each of the Australian blast-furnaces, in New South Wales, Tasmania, Victoria and South Australia, has an archaeology which must place it in a local environment, inside a local society, as an employer of men, a builder of settlements, a catalyst in communications and a small market force, not simply as an example of an inadequate technology or an inferior management which inevitably failed. The colonial iron industry was in some measure a

The first hot blast-furnace in Australia, at Redbill Point, Tasmania, completed in 1875. It was the only nineteenth-century furnace in Australia to have a vertical hoist for raising ore, flux and fuel to the loading platform. (*Illustrated Australian News*, no. 232, 29 December 1875, p. 204)

This furnace at Standish in the Adirondacks, New York State, built in 1885–6, looks state-of-the-art, but was still burning charcoal. Otherwise it closely resembles Sandford's 1907 furnace at Lithgow. (Adirondack Museum, P47859)

statement of aspirations towards greater national self-sufficiency, an inverted commentary on the state of the iron industry in Britain, a series of experiments heightening the Australian consciousness of its raw resources, sharpening the appraisal of geological exploration and leading in what finally became a straight line of progression to Lithgow, Newcastle, Port Kembla and Whyalla.

FIRST BLAST:
THE FITZROY IRONWORKS
AT MITTAGONG,
NEW SOUTH WALES

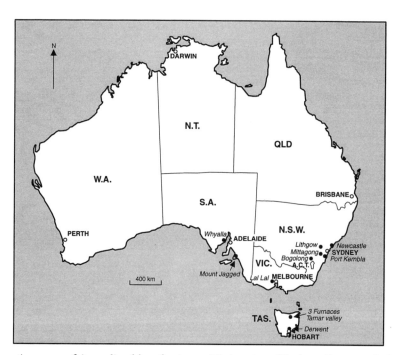

Location map of Australian blast-furnaces. (University of Sydney Cartography)

The site of the blast-furnace at Mittagong is an icon for the Australian iron industry. It is here that native Australian ores were first shown to be feasible sources of locally smelted pig-iron. Little attempt was made to investigate systematically the availability of iron ore in New South Wales during the first half-century of European settlement, as was not the case with the state's coal reserves.

Foundries had flourished in New South Wales, using pig-iron imported from Britain, which they increasingly supplemented with recycled scrap-iron from Australian sites. By the 1830s there were quite sizeable foundries in Sydney, such as William Browne's in Sussex Street. In 1840 Browne had a 5-horsepower engine, a drilling machine, a very expensive boring mill and a newly imported turning lathe on a bed 7 metres long; while in his casting-room he had a furnace assisted by a large pair of bellows and an overhead crane to transport the ladles, the mould-boxes and the castings with greater economy of labour.[1]

The need for iron goods was self-evident in a colony born during the Industrial Revolution. The expanding population and the increasing complexity of social needs created demand, so iron objects and iron components, great and small, were part of everyone's consciousness. The range of locally made iron products grew steadily as nails and horseshoes were made by Australian blacksmiths and by the 1830s large industrial equipment such as boilers were produced in Australian foundries. Whereas John Dickson had imported a steam-engine and boiler for his Darling Harbour mill in 1815, 20 years later the boiler for the coal-mines on Tasman Peninsula was manufactured in Hobart. An increasing proportion of local needs, both for

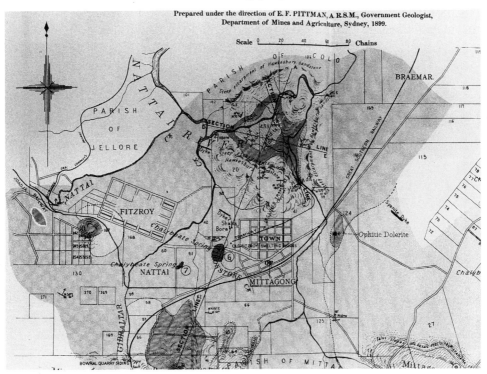

Ironstone deposits (6, 7) at Mittagong. (Map by E. F. Pittman, 1899, printed in J. B. Jaquet, *Iron Ore Deposits of New South Wales*, 1901)

business and for government, was being met by local entrepreneurs.

As a result, the discovery of an iron ore deposit at Mittagong by the government surveyor in 1833 did not go unnoticed. The deposit was substantial, of apparently good quality, and it was conveniently sited beside the Great South Road. Indeed, it was actually cut into by the final alignment of Thomas Mitchell's road running from Mittagong to Berrima. The bridge built across Gibbergunyah Creek was known as Iron Stone Bridge,[2] although the major ore deposit lies 300 metres east of the bridge.

Capital, vision, technical knowledge and optimism were needed before the Mittagong ore could be smelted on site. Two years before the gold-rush, a combination of business interests took the first decisive step to establish an iron-smelting industry in Australia.

A group headed by a local landholder, John Thomas Neale, backed by Sydney money, opened the smelter in 1848—the investors were tempted by the combination of raw materials available at Mittagong. The iron ore deposit literally lay on the main road. The adjacent area was still heavily wooded, despite some pastoral clearances, so charcoal might be produced as fuel without substantial cartage problems. The Catalan furnace erected quickly in 1848 was designed for charcoal and worked effectively.[3] Although the first manager, Mr Povey, dug some limestone out near the works, there was no immediate need to find a major deposit to act as a flux because, as F. J. Rothery reported in 1854, the Mittagong ores 'are readily reduced to the metallic state—and the earthy matter, with which they are combined,

The spade and wheelbarrow made partly from iron smelted at Fitzroy being used at the inauguration of the Sydney to Parramatta railway, July 1850. (Engraving by W. Harris. Privately owned: another copy in ML, SSVI/RA1/1)

forms a glass or slag, *without the addition of a flux*. Mr Morgan [the British mining engineer who examined the ore in 1852] states that he had never met with Ores, where the earthy matter had so slight a tendency to enter into combination with the Metal, when reduced'.[4]

This simple operation of heating the local red hematite ore with locally produced charcoal created good quality iron and the publicity received by the first manufactured products in 1848–50 was good for morale, although the quantity was insufficient for profit. Some of these emotive manufactures survive. One of them is of double significance, since it is the spade made from Mittagong iron used in December 1850 to turn the first sod for the Sydney to Parramatta railway. This spade was treasured for its railway associations rather than its metallurgical interest and survives in the State Rail Authority archive in Sydney.

When Governor Fitzroy visited the ironworks in March 1850, fifty small castings of a lion rampant were distributed as souvenirs. Two of these distinguished casts survive at the public school in Pioneer Street, Mittagong, and a third is in the Mittagong Bowling Club in Alfred Street. No doubt others survive elsewhere, for they are highly collectible pieces of Australiana. They are also evidence for the small quantity of iron being produced at the blast-furnace. The first thing that anyone who has seen a photograph of a Fitzroy lion says when confronted with the real thing, usually the one above the school entrance, is 'How small!'.

The Catalan forge did not survive, and only its products, the lions and the spade, are material testimony to its effectiveness. Unlike the pig-iron from later blast-furnaces, the iron from this first stage at Mittagong was in the form of a bloom. Some blooms weighing a total of 250 tonnes had been produced between 1848 and 1852, when the trip-hammer which produced the wrought iron from the large blooms met with an accident.

The fuel was exclusively timber, charcoal being supplemented by green timber; but coal was actively sought by the company in the seams which could best be mined in the Nattai Gorge, where they outcropped, or, initially, some thirty kilometres away at Black Bob's Creek. Fuel supplies remained a problem throughout the 40 years of Fitzroy's existence and the need to keep cartage costs to a minimum led to the creation of two separate tramway systems to the Nattai Gorge and the unsuccessful sinking of a deep shaft close to the works themselves.[5] The quality of the coal in this furthest extension of the Illawarra coal deposits caused concern: it could not be used for coke and it was not ideal for smelting.

The iron ore deposit itself, beside the main road, formed the lower part of what is now Mineral Springs reserve. It was partly open-cut, like the later mines at Mount Vulcan and Ilfracombe in Tasmania or Lal Lal in Victoria, but also had a 'naturally formed adit, entered from the bank on the road-side'

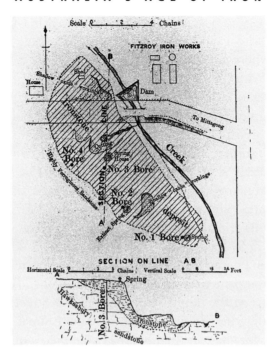

Plan and section of the iron ore deposit beside Fitzroy ironworks and straddling the main south road. (J. B. Jaquet, *Iron Ore Deposits of New South Wales*, 1901, p. 51)

opening out into 'various chambers'.[6] No traces of either adit or open-cut remain at Fitzroy, in contrast to the fine quarries in Tasmania and Victoria.

Unlike at the other plants, the ore at Fitzroy was roasted in the open air, just beside the road, burning on stacks of wood and coal to remove water and other extraneous matter. This process continued for a long time: it is well described by the *Sydney Morning Herald* in 1865, and the calcining stack of ore is very clear in a photograph taken in the early 1870s (see p. 20).[7]

All this belonged to subsequent stages of technology. After the trip-hammer fractured in the early 1850s, iron ore continued to be quarried but was sent to Peter Nicol Russell's foundry at Pyrmont in Sydney. The company was re-formed as the Fitz Roy Iron and Coal Mining Company. A syndicate then built rolling-mills in 1859 and in the following year became incorporated as the Fitzroy Iron Works Company. The new manager, B. W. Lattin, created a blast-furnace complex in 1863–4.[8]

There were two quite distinct phases in the iron-making operation at Mittagong. There is now no trace of the Catalan forge, where the early wrought-iron was produced. Even the precise site is uncertain. In the second phase beginning in 1863 a colonial ironworks was built to a design already old-fashioned in Britain, but with an expectation of converting to the more efficient hot blast as soon as possible. With cold blast it was hoped to produce up to 120 tonnes of pig-iron a week; with hot blast an increase to 200 tonnes of pig from 400 tonnes of ore, 300 tonnes of coal and 60 tonnes of limestone was anticipated in 1864.[9]

The management of Lattin and the company direction were both ineffective. Financial records were as inadequate as technological control and when a new company took over in 1864 under the leadership of Ebenezer Vickery, it soon found hidden dimensions to the obvious problems on site. Lattin left and was replaced by J. K. Hampshire as manager. Vickery, a Cornish Methodist and a very successful investor and entrepreneur both in Sydney and in rural New South Wales, brought a new vigour to the board of directors. Vickery had come to Australia at the age of six in 1833 and he took over his father's boot factory in George Street, Sydney, in 1851 while his father concentrated on acquiring country properties. Vickery acquired premises in Pitt Street in 1860 and reconstructed them as Vickery's Chambers using iron girders from Fitzroy in 1864. It is characteristic of Vickery that his chambers should be innovative: they were the first Australian building to use iron in this way. His subsequent career lay partly in shipping and partly in coal-mining in the Illawarra, while he inherited and purchased a great deal of real estate in the metropolitan area and in New South Wales at large. He was a commanding figure in the business and pastoral world as well as in evangelical Methodism.[10] If anyone could succeed at Fitzroy it was Ebenezer Vickery.

The dimensions of Vickery's frustrations at Mittagong are fully documented in the minute-book of the Fitzroy Iron Works Company during the period of his chairmanship, from 1864 to 1872. This minute-book of 380 pages has been preserved in the Vickery family but only came to light in mid-1992 when Mr Brian Rogers of the University of Wollongong was seeking documentation on one of Vickery's Illawarra collieries. It affords a uniquely detailed insight into the development of Fitzroy and into some of the inscrutable stone-cut foundations surviving from the 1860s and 1870s.

Unlike many company directors, Vickery often visited the works and made personal reports to the board from time to time. On 14 October 1864, he reported the unworkable condition of Lattin's blast-furnace: 'The Blast Furnace exhibits an appearance of having come to grief. The lower part is completely gutted—the fire-bricks used were evidently bad in quality and defectively placed, very costly though effective drains are being excavated out of the solid rock under and at the back of the Blast Furnace and are almost completed.'[11] This drainage channel, hard against the steep slope to the east of the present foundations, is very clear, and still operates; it is of critical importance in helping to fix the location of the 1860s blast-furnace in relation to the total site.

The blast-furnace was partly rebuilt, with a new fire-brick interior, in

October 1864. The need for a hot-air blast was recognized, vigorous action was initiated and a great deal of money was spent. The inventory of the entire plant made in September 1864 shows that the blast-furnace was then powered by a 25-horsepower engine and that there were three boilers in the blast-furnace complex. A beam-engine was used, presumably for the cold blast. There were five rolling-mills, three for general purpose merchant bars, two for sheet iron, powered by one 50-horsepower engine. There was a

Fitzroy ironworks as it was under Ebenezer Vickery in the 1860s. A heap of iron ore and fuel for calcining in the open air is in the front right beside the main south road. (Photograph early 1870s, reproduced in Mittagong Iron Week Celebrations Committee, *Centenary of Australia's First Iron Smelting at Mittagong, New South Wales*, Mittagong 1948, p. 12).

Open-air calcining of ore in the eighteenth century. The 'truncated quadrangular pyramid' of ore and wood is similar to that shown at Fitzroy a century later. (Diderot, *Recueil des Planches*, 5me livraison, vol. 6, 1768, Mineralogie, Calcination des Mines, plate 1, fig. 1)

stockpile of 1500 tonnes of iron ore already calcined in the open air, together with 60 tonnes of pig-iron, previously smelted. In the foundry there were two furnaces for melting scrap-iron and a crane was used for the two large ladles of hot metal, while the six smaller ladles were carried to the moulding boxes by hand. Bricks could be made using the clay mill. A railway had been constructed to the nearest coal-mine in Nattai Gorge, but general reliance for transport was placed on wheelbarrows and horse-drawn drays.[12]

Vickery was, of course, aware that the railway was being extended southwards. The tunnel through The Gib between Mittagong and Bowral was completed in 1866 and the railway station in Mittagong opened in 1867 on land offered by the Fitzroy iron company. Therefore, the potential for greatly increased sales through better communications continued to encourage Vickery to spend heavily on the ironworks. He was supported in this by Simon Zollner, another director, who ran a very successful galvanized-iron works in Sydney (on the site of Dickson's Mill in Sussex Street) and had a clear interest in obtaining locally produced iron at a competitive price.

As well as reconstructing the interior of the blast-furnace, Vickery and Zollner brought the tramway that ran to the Nattai coal-mine back into operation; started to sink a shaft-mine close to the works to supersede the 2 kilometres of haulage from the Nattai adits; bought new equipment such as an expensive lathe; pressed ahead with the conversion to hot blast; and 'consented to a rearrangement of the entire works, they being formerly arranged in such a way as to make every production trebly expensive and to render proper oversight an impossibility'—so a new cupola, new workshops, a new foundry and a more powerful crane were all installed.[13] It is this rearranged plant that is shown on all surviving illustrations.

The only really successful year for this new plant was 1865, but even the well-known casting of the metal cylinders for the bridge over the Murrumbidgee at Gundagai was only achieved after embarrassing failures: the first castings early in 1865 'had proved a failure owing to there not being sufficient metal in the Cupola to complete the same'.[14] It is far from clear that this iron in fact came from locally smelted pig at all, for the blast-furnace was not relit until 2 May 1865, the new hot-air blast was turned on the following morning and the first 3.5 tonnes of iron were tapped late that evening in 83 pigs, with a further 5 tonnes on 4 May.[15] Vickery and Zollner were concerned that the supply of coal was inadequate but there was general relief and optimism.

Ominous signs were still present, however. In June 1865, the quality of the anthracite fuel was being implicitly criticized and the stonework on the blast-furnace itself was working loose.[16] The foundry was too small, the hot blast engine-room too cluttered, the coal-shaft took a long time to sink and never produced any suitable coal in any quantity. The furnace never reached the anticipated production of 100 tonnes of pig-iron a week; the pig-iron did not sell unless made into bars and castings in the Fitzroy rolling-mills, which were over-strained and there was a great need of puddling furnaces. The Board was told on 7 August 1865 that £10000 was needed as further investment,[17] and over the next two years a further share float, then a government subsidy, were sought.

Zollner drew attention to Bessemer's process for steel on the basis of a London *Times* report of Bessemer's address to the British Association for the Advancement of Science in 1865, but no action was taken.[18] The only technical book in the company offices at Mittagong was the fourth edition of Andrew Ure's *Dictionary of Arts, Manufactures and Mines*, published in 1853. Ure had been the teacher of James Neilson, who patented hot blast for iron-smelters in 1828, and the furnace which Ure discusses at length with seven sections and elevations is remarkably similar to the form which Fitzroy took in the mid-1860s.[19]

On the foundry side of Fitzroy, new expertise and wide experience were to be brought to the plant by the acceptance of Peter Nicol Russell's Sydney engineering firm into partnership at the end of 1865.[20] John Russell was named as managing director at Mittagong with George Russell superintending the Sydney business. The brochure advertising these changes in January 1866 also sought more capital to build two more blast-furnaces and to extend the rolling-mills with a view to the government contract for rails.[21] But by 22 February 1866 the prospectus had failed to bring in new capital, P. N. Russell and Co. had withdrawn from the amalgamation and the new rolling-mills were still not working.[22] Zollner reported on the closure of the plant on 21 April 1866 and the unsuitability of the stockpiled pig-iron for the still incomplete order for Gundagai Bridge. The remaining cylinders for the bridge were to be supplied by P. N. Russell instead, so the largest and most prestigious order at Fitzroy could not be met.[23]

A petition to the governor for government assistance in May 1867 gave a convenient summary of the achievements of the smelting operation under Vickery and Zollner:

> It was now an established fact that they could make iron. They had smelted 5000 tons, and had manufactured nearly 3000 tons, some of which had been sent to England, and some to California, and they had received the most satisfactory reports as to its quality . . . No other undertaking in the colony . . . had such claims upon the Government as the iron works. A large population would be employed, railway traffic would be created, Crown lands in the vicinity of the mines, which were now unsaleable, would then find a ready market, and the revenue in a variety of ways would be benefited.

In response to questions from the premier, James Martin, Vickery sought £30000 to build new furnaces and rolling-mills within 12 months and claimed that 'for two years between 600 and 700 people (including the wives and families) had been employed on the works'.[24]

The appeal for government assistance failed. Vickery and Zollner appointed a new manager from Newport in Wales, and Thomas Levick arrived in the colony in December 1867.[25] But the persistent preoccupation with sinking the shaft adjacent to the blast-furnace to tap the anticipated coal-seam far below was Vickery's most expensive mistake. In January 1868 Levick organized an interesting and thorough report on the coal deposits and the quality of the iron ore, expressing surprise that the ore had normally been roasted before smelting.[26]

Much more serious were Levick's findings about the construction of the blast-furnace:

> The Blast Furnace is built very substantially but from some cause the base has been cracked and the arch in the front of the Furnace given way, probably from the expansion of the Interior Brickwork and from there not being a space between it and the lining or perhaps by not allowing the lining sufficient time to dry thoroughly: before blowing in the Furnace a Fire ought to be kept in the Hearth for from 6 weeks to 2 months before blowing in: also with a massive Stone Casing holes ought to have been left at intervals to allow any moisture to escape.[27]

The lack of a clay packing between fire-bricks and stone cladding, successfully incorporated into the design of the Lal Lal blast-furnace in 1880, was a very serious defect indeed at Fitzroy.

Levick was critical of the old-fashioned design of the hot-blast stove and the lack of any back-up should it fail; and the pipes were liable to crack, he commented. The blast-main, carrying the hot air from the stove to the furnace, was criticized for being underground, making it possible 'that the slag might run back through the tuyeres into the main'.[28] The channel cut into bedrock which carried the blast-main up to 1868 was one of the most puzzling features of the present foundations until Levick's report explained its purpose. Since his advice was acted upon, all photographs and lithographs of the plant in the 1870s show an above-ground blast-main.

The main was therefore to be rebuilt. The blast-furnace itself had substantial repairs to one of the stone arches on the lower furnace; the slag and iron were removed from the well just as Dubois had to do at Mount Jagged six years later; and the furnace had to be relined with fire-bricks made on the property up to the angle of the boshes.[29] A new fire-clay mill ordered in April 1868 was completed in July.[30] Enoch Hughes and his brother Andrew leased the rolling-mills to manufacture the stockpiled pig-iron but this was unsuccessful and the Hughes brothers withdrew in mid-year.[31] The crisis over coal for the smelter was not resolved by buying supplies from Cataract colliery near Berrima and the hope that the extension of the railway would

Fitzroy blast-furnace soon after closure, photographed by W. J. Crawley of Mittagong *circa* 1880. This view from the north is the best surviving: it shows the materials store to the left, the square chimney stack beyond the loading bridge, the blowing-house between the stack and the blast-furnace, the furnace itself, the open-sided casting-shed roofed with curved iron and part of the foundry to the right. (Berrima and District Historical Society, E28/1)

make cheaper the transport of limestone from the Marulan quarries to Mittagong was deferred.

With some difficulty, the furnace was repaired late in 1868. The entire lower part of the brick interior had to be replaced, while the upper part was propped up. Masonry was taken down and replaced on the lower furnace and two broken tie-bolts holding the masonry together were, with difficulty, replaced. So shaky was the whole structure that some of the passages through the masonry piers had to be filled up.

Since the fire-clay on the property was not proving as successful as expected, Levick proposed to use slabs of quartz sandstone in the hearth of the blast-furnace. This use of fire-stone instead of fire-brick in the hearth of a furnace was also the strategy employed at Ilfracombe five years later: fire-stone slabs were exported to Tasmania from Garnkirk in Scotland. The stone used at Fitzroy was local. As Levick explained to the board of directors, 'this material is always employed for the bottom and sides of the hearth where it can be obtained so that it is no new experiment. The great advantage for the hearth is that the stone can be got in very large blocks & consequently the joints are fewer than could be made with brickwork'.[32]

The advantage of this smoother surface can still be seen at Ilfracombe, where the hearth is exposed. Another example of the technique is the floor of an intact calcining kiln on the Grose Valley escarpment in the Blue Mountains of New South Wales, below Asgard Swamp. At Asgard Swamp, however, the slabs were manufactured from a clay mixture, in which a dog impressed its paws before the paving-stone hardened.[33] At Fitzroy it seems that the sandstone was simply cut, which may explain why at Fitzroy, and not elsewhere, the floor of the hearth was protected by a layer of fire-bricks. This combination would be sufficient, it was hoped, to withstand the pressures within the furnace.

Despite these necessary steps, which were supported by Ebenezer Vickery and Simon Zollner, everything failed. Levick resigned on the grounds of ill health on 28 June 1869; the new furnacemen imported from Wales at company expense arrived just as everything was closing and were paid to return to Britain. Vickery in an uncharacteristically anguished report on 30 July concluded: 'Thus crippled and embarrassed it is impossible further to develop the resources and wealth of the property and stay the daily increasing individual liability of the Shareholders.'[34] The board resolved to wind up the Fitzroy Iron Works Company at its meeting held on 29 November 1869 and one of the directors, John Frazer, bought all the assets of the company for a mere £10 000 in January 1870.[35] The shareholders were liable for the outstanding debts totalling £12 500, but by judicious sale of remaining assets, this was reduced to £1420 and the board met for the last time on 28 October 1872.[36]

Although the company chaired by Ebenezer Vickery relinquished the iron-making plant, Vickery and a number of his colleagues retained an interest in Mittagong. They bought some of Fitzroy's land and were vitally involved in the development of the company town known as New Sheffield.

Relationship of Fitzroy ironworks to the company town of New Sheffield and the government town of Fitzroy. (University of Sydney Cartography)

New Sheffield is the north-east sector of modern Mittagong, east of the ironworks and north of the highway, bounded by the sharply rising heights of Mount Alexandra to the north of Leopold Street. The creation of the Mittagong Land Company Ltd in December 1883, with Vickery a founding director,[37] conceals the long-term association of the iron company of the 1860s with town development. Very soon after the creation of the Fitzroy Iron Works Company, the board, with Vickery in the chair, had decided to develop 100 acres (40 hectares) as a company town. On 26 August 1864 Vickery and five other directors, including Zollner and John Frazer (who bought the works in 1872), debated how a model township should be created.[38] The master plan evolved at that meeting, held in Mittagong, was put into effect and is still the basic structure of that part of Mittagong today. The new town, named New Sheffield at the August meeting, balanced the government town of Fitzroy (now known as Welby) to the west of the iron-works. The government town followed the regular grid pattern. New Sheffield looked rather different. The portions were each a quarter-acre and were conceived as workers', managerial and general housing. Reflecting Vickery's strong religious interests, the company laid aside a whole acre in a central position for a Wesleyan church and paid for the building in 1865. A large square to the north of the church was reserved for public recreation (and is now occupied by the bowling club). Unlike Fitzroy (Welby), New Sheffield was arranged in streets 20 metres broad alternating with lanes 10 metres broad running east–west; the north–south crossroads were all 20 metres broad. This created a townscape very different from most country towns and strikingly different from Welby or from the later much closer sub-division of Nattai between the Great South Road and the railway. The iron-works played, therefore, a critically important role in producing Mittagong's rather strange urban design.

Because of the uncertain future of the ironworks, few permanent houses were built in New Sheffield, although most of the portions were sold in the 1860s. So when the Mittagong Land Company was formed in 1883 there was considerable scope for further sales and some reorganization of portions in New Sheffield. The auction of 1884 aroused a great deal of interest and over the next 10 years a new sort of Mittagong resident built houses both in stone and brick which enhance the area still. Since the sale plan of 1884[39] showed the location of existing houses, a comparison of the relative success of the Mittagong Land Company with the relative failure of the Fitzroy Iron Works Company as urban entrepreneurs can be more easily made. But the continuity represented by Ebenezer Vickery is a concealed element in the 30 years of town creation. It is no accident that the railway station of 1867 was located on company land immediately south of New Sheffield; its distance from the government town of Fitzroy (Welby) did nothing to assist that town

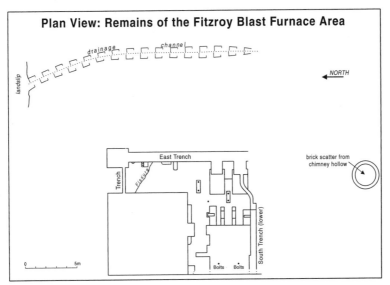

Fitzroy ironworks, plan of foundations of blast-furnaces and casting-floor (on left) and blowing-engine-house (on right). (Patricia Thams and University of Sydney Cartography)

Fitzroy ironworks: rock-cut foundations of blowing-engine-house, from west. (R. Ian Jack, 1992)

to grow and all the gain was to the successive developers of the ironworks initiative.

Both New Sheffield and the remains of the blast-furnace site reflect the policies implemented by Vickery in the 1860s. The group of industrial buildings on an artificial terrace sloping upwards against a steep but low hill to the east is represented now by levelled bedrock and by a number of rock-cuttings: for drainage, for the original location of the blast-main, for the footings of the various engines and pieces of equipment such as lathes. The blast-furnace itself was systematically demolished 65 years ago and the stone machine house was partly re-erected in 1911 as a hall adjacent to the nearby School of Arts. As a result of the placing of a remarkably unsuitable memorial in trachyte by the Royal Australian Historical Society and BHP in 1948, the foundations of the furnace and the casting-shed on the shelving rock immediately to the west have been obscured, but the position of the furnace is ascertainable by its relationship to the blowing-house foundation, the rock-cut drain and the brick scatter at the site of the chimney stack beyond to the south. The trestle-bridge from the top of the hill to the mouth of the furnace has left no obvious footings but its position is clear from coal scatter on a restricted part of the steep slope and fallen debris across the drain.

The materials storage sheds for the new furnace were on top of the hill to the east. A trestle-bridge led from the hill across to the loading openings in the top of the furnace. By 1863 it had been decided to use only coal or coke as fuel and the original optimism of the 1850s that no flux was needed for the ore had been replaced by a regular use of limestone from the huge deposits 50 kilometres away at Marulan. So coal, limestone and iron ore were stored in sheds just to the west of Pioneer Street.

The storage area is not discernible today. Nor is the tramway which raised

The horse tramway from Fitzroy ironworks to its coal adits in Nattai Gorge. (*Illustrated Sydney News*, 15 April 1869, p. 169; courtesy National Library of Australia)

ore from the mine just across the road and limestone brought in by horse-dray from Marulan along the south road, so that it could be stored near the furnace feeder.

What has left instructive and unexpected remains is the tramway from the company's principal coal-mine in Nattai Gorge. The successive companies at Fitzroy used various sources of coal, most of them tapping the local seams, but at mines as far apart as Black Bob's Creek and Cataract (north of Berrima) as well as Nattai Gorge and the ironworks site itself. The shafts sunk on the property in 1865 to reach the seam at some seventy metres have not been located, but the adits into the outcrop of the seams on the face of Nattai Gorge and the tramways connecting them with the works 2 kilometres away have left evocative traces.

The major adit of the early mine in the gorge was destroyed in 1989 by the massive road-works of the Mittagong bypass. One of the construction workers on the approaches to the new Nattai River bridge recalls how the bulldozers revealed a tunnel about one and a half metres square with pit-props intact; but no one was informed and no records were kept. This adit of the 1860s was reached by a relatively level tramway running on the line of the present navigable roadway from the north-east corner of Mittagong round the east side of Mount Alexandra down to the convulsive road-works in the gorge.

In 1874 British investors, including an engineer, David Smith, decided to reinvestigate the coal situation prior to the reopening of the ironworks after the four-year closure. The new Fitzroy Bessemer Steel, Hematite, Iron & Coal Co. built an entirely new tramway to Nattai Gorge and probably opened a new adit there after deciding that the coal was suitable after all. This tramway, unlike its predecessor, went straight over Mount Alexandra, with a long steady climb up from the north of New Sheffield, and then going across a gully, through a rock face and finally plunging down an incline into the Nattai Gorge itself. To operate this new track of some two kilometres a winding engine was installed at the highest point. The iron bolts for the base of the engine are still in place on a levelled part of the rocky summit. Immediately below the engine base a semicircular housing for the 4-metre fly-wheel was carved out of the living rock face and below that steps were carved into a sump-hole in the rock. The tramway ran past this rock face through a narrow cutting and almost immediately must have used a trestle-bridge to cross the gully. Beyond the gully, to the north, a tunnel 200 metres long was cut through the rock. Beyond the tunnel there was an extensive rock overhang, which gave shelter in bad weather, and a flat area was provided at the head of the incline. The track went down steeply for about 300 metres to the earlier tramway which curved round the gorge to the west to reach at least six adits.[40] These adits lay between Gibbergunyah

The 1874 tramway from Fitzroy to Nattai Gorge coal-mine was powered by a steam-engine atop Mount Alexandra: the rock-cutting for the fly-wheel is still a striking feature. Scale in 20-centimetre intervals. (R. Ian Jack, 1992)

The tunnel at the head of the 1874 incline down to Fitzroy's coal-mine in Nattai Gorge taken from the south. (R. Ian Jack, 1992)

Creek on the west and the great bend in the Nattai River to the east and all are close to the swathe made by the Mittagong bypass. It is both difficult and hazardous to establish whether all suffered the fate of the one described by the construction worker.

What *is* clear, however, is that an elaborate and ingenious tramway system employing gravitational balances between skips rising from the mines to Mount Alexandra and skips descending from Mount Alexandra to the Fitzroy ironworks was successfully installed, using a steam-powered winding engine as the prime mover at the highest point.

Despite all this work, the new tramway was barely used. It could not have been in operation before late 1874, since Berrima coal was purchased throughout that year, and it was not used after 1875 when a new manager, David Lawson, succeeded David Smith.[41] Lawson decided that the Nattai coal was unsuitable by itself and he apparently did not favour mixing it with Berrima or Bulli coal as Smith had probably done. For the remaining year of active smelting at Fitzroy, all coal came first from Bulli, where excellent coking coal was produced, or in 1877 from the Cataract mine at Berrima. In March 1877 the Fitzroy smelter went out of blast and never resumed.

The rolling-mills continued, as they were to do at Eskbank in Lithgow. At Fitzroy there was an accumulation of some 1000 tonnes of pig-iron and, of course, every rolling-mill was anxious to recycle scrap-iron. The stockpile of pig-iron at Mittagong was rolled into rails for the new railway from Mittagong to the kerosene shale-mines and plant in Joadja Creek valley some fifteen kilometres away.

Very little is usually said about the rolling-mill section of the Fitzroy works. As at Lithgow, however, the puddling furnaces, foundries and rolling-mills were the mainstay of the enterprise: they could keep in operation, using scrap-iron or stockpiled pig, during the recurrent periods of uncertainty at the blast-furnace. Other than the earliest rolling-mills, most of the heavy equipment used in the foundry was cast on site, some of it from local ore. After problems with badly laid foundations for some of the machinery, which involved expensive re-laying in 1876, the last major job undertaken at the rolling-mill was the manufacture of the Joadja railway in 1878, but the plant remained and was used by William Sandford for nine months in 1886–7 and was again remodelled abortively by an English firm, Lambert Bros, in 1896.[42]

The last smelting of the Mittagong ore was done by a local engineer, William Brazenall, who used a small furnace between 1889 and 1891. He displayed castings from this pig-iron at the Mining Exhibition in London and won a first prize. The cast-iron lace on the front verandah of three of the houses built in New Sheffield after the Land Company's sale is stamped W. BRAZENALL: these houses, 24 Edward Lane and 1 and 3 Queen Street, seem therefore to display castings from the very last smeltings of local ore.

The Brazenall verandah columns have not been recognized as local work, but the town retains a pride in the few examples of Fitzroy castings: a lamp-post in the grounds of the Anglican church, two more lamp-posts bizarrely inserted into the blast-furnace foundations, and one of the Fitzroy lions cast in 1850 displayed over the public school entrance in Pioneer Street. Lake Alexandra, which occupies the north-west section of New Sheffield, is also remembered as the final effort to supply adequate water to the works in the 1870s.

Fitzroy was a failure, but recurrent attempts to make it viable sustained a vision of a native iron industry from the 1840s until the 1870s. The last attempt to make Fitzroy successful came in the mid-1870s, just as Tasmania, South Australia and Victoria opened blast-furnaces in a changed international economy.

CHAPTER TWO

SMELTING BESIDE
THE TAMAR

Colonial Australia was a child of the Industrial Revolution. Although British governments did not encourage any precocious self-sufficiency in manufactures throughout its dependencies, early Australian settlers were highly conscious of the potential value of basic raw materials. In New South Wales, surface traces of coal were observed just south of Newcastle as early as 1791, near Port Stephens five years later and on the Illawarra coast in 1797, culminating in the major Newcastle discoveries in 1800–1.[1] Coal samples were routinely sent back to Britain for appraisal in the first decades of settlement, and in 1802 the former governor, John Hunter, commented: 'There are so many specimens of this [New South Wales] coal in England that its qualities are known and, I believe, considered very fine.' Hunter went on to moot a potential iron-smelting industry, founded on the coking potential of the Newcastle coal. 'I apprehend,' he wrote, 'the cinders, after the tar is extracted, would answer every purpose of an iron foundry, which might be carried on to any extent Government wished, the country abounding with so much of that ore.'[2]

Hunter in 1802 knew nothing of the iron resources of Tasmania. Lieutenant Bowen established his settlement at Risdon Cove only in September 1803 and the first shipload of convicts and soldiers to settle in Northern Tasmania landed in the Tamar estuary in the following spring.

The successive attempts in 1804–5 to find a suitable township site on the Tamar, first at George Town on the east bank, then at York Town on the opposite side on West Arm, and finally, late in 1805, at Launceston, gave opportunity and incentive to explore and assess the country along the Tamar estuary. During this initial process of discovery, outcrops of iron ore were discovered in the area of Mount Vulcan, only 6 kilometres due south of York Town; and in 1805 a quantity of iron ore was mined and dispatched to Sydney.[3]

Samples of this Tasmanian ore were sent on to England, just as New South Wales coal had been sent over the past decade. The ironstone was said to have produced some 70 per cent of iron in English smelters, an unbelievably high yield. But no systematic iron-mining occurred. Convicts might have been dispatched in iron gangs to Mount Vulcan, as they later were (under a changing penal philosophy) to the coal-mines on Tasman Peninsula, but Lieutenant-Governor Paterson did no more in 1805 and 1806 than write about the possibility and note the advantages of the Tamar for ocean transport.[4]

With the creation of Launceston and the redevelopment of George Town after 1819, good land on both sides of the Tamar was increasingly exploited by farmers, and the iron ore in the western hills was not forgotten. John Oxley's mind ran on establishing foundries in the area in 1811,[5] and George William Evans, writing a description of the island about 1819, was able to give a glowing account of the potential of the iron deposits. The English testings of Tamar ore samples 13 years earlier had not been forgotten and more systematic exploration had established the location of the more visible outcrops.

'Within a few miles of Launceston, there is a most surprising abundance of iron,' Evans remarked. 'Literally speaking, there are entire mountains of this ore, which is so remarkably rich that it has been found to yield seventy per cent of pure metal.'[6] Evans noted that these iron deposits on Mount Vulcan and the other hills around Anderson's Creek had not yet been worked, but he was optimistic that they would become 'at no very remote period, a source of considerable wealth to [the area's] inhabitants'.[7] As William Mann shrewdly observed in the 1830s, however, 'until the population becomes more dense, they will be better employed in pastoral and agricultural pursuits, than in working mines'.[8]

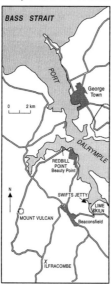

Location map of ironworks in the Tamar Valley of North Tasmania. (University of Sydney Cartography)

Mann thought that the cheapness of British manufactured goods would stifle local colonial enterprise 'for centuries to come'. In fact a combination of factors encouraged Australian entrepreneurs to create a local iron industry in Tasmania before forty years had elapsed.

The elements in this rapid change of attitude were partly local to Tasmania, partly international on a broad economic and commercial spectrum. The factors which were specific to North Tasmania were threefold: the successful commercial smelting of Tasmanian ore overseas; the awareness of suitable limestone deposits near to the ironstone; and professional geological appraisal.

The shipping of a quantity of Tamar ore to Scotland in 1860 and its subsequent return in the form of cast-iron railings constituted a major stage in awakening commercial consciousness. The ore came from a deposit at Ilfracombe. Although the name 'Ilfracombe' was attached to a wider area than just the Middle Arm Creek system south-east of the Anderson's Creek deposits, it seems almost certain that the present property of Ilfracombe was the source of this ore in 1860. The establishment of a timber business there was the catalyst. A tramway from the sawmill to a wharf on the Tamar at the present Beauty Point, 11 kilometres away, was constructed in 1857. It was a happy coincidence that an excellent iron deposit lay only 500 metres away from the sawmill and, although the Ilfracombe Saw Mills and Railway Company had no mandate to mine iron, it is clear that the ore deposit was prospected and substantial samples of easily accessible ore were sent out on

ST. JOHN ST., LAUNCESTON.

Railings cast in Scotland from Ilfracombe iron ore smelted in Lanarkshire and erected outside the government building in Launceston in 1860. (Postcard *c.* 1890; Queen Victoria Museum and Art Gallery, Launceston, P539)

the timber tramway. In 1873, six or seven years after the sawmill had closed, a blast-furnace was built close to the iron ore outcrop and the decayed tramway became the property of the iron company. In the late 1850s, however, the initiative taken by sawmillers in exporting the ore made possible a highly public demonstration of future smelting potential.

The Ilfracombe iron ore was sent to Scotland, where it was smelted in Lanarkshire by the great Shotts Iron Company of Edinburgh and cast into superb railings, which were shipped back to Tasmania and erected in Launceston in 1860. The railings were very public indeed, for they stood on three sides of the new government building at the north-east corner of Paterson and St John streets. Two bays of railings faced Paterson Street, thirteen bays and three gates St John Street, in the heart of Launceston. Each bay was almost three and a half metres long, the dividing iron pillars (stamped by Shotts) were 2.3 metres high and the gates were 1.3 metres wide.

Not only were these railings highly visible to everyone who visited Launceston on official or commercial business, but they also featured in many early photographs and, ultimately, on postcards. The earliest of the photographs to survive was taken in the 1860s and shows the railings clearly. The doubts which have been expressed by Coultman Smith about the possibility of so early a date for the speculative mining of Ilfracombe iron ore are unjustified.[9] This is in sharp contrast to the analogous story about the use of Lal Lal iron ore by the Union Foundry in Ballarat to make the railings of St Patrick's Cathedral there in 1865–8; there is no reason to believe that Lal Lal iron ore (unlike Lal Lal lignite and gold) was mined before 1874 and the story linking St Patrick's with local iron ore developed later.[10] In Tasmania the linkages, though partly circumstantial, are far more secure between Ilfracombe and Shotts Foundry.

In the Tamar district, the story of how the Launceston railings came to be cast in 1860 was not forgotten (whereas in Ballarat the story of St Patrick's railings was manufactured). After 78 years the government buildings of Launceston lost their railings to relieve congestion on the busy pavements of St John and Paterson streets. The government buildings remained (and are at the time of writing the Tasmanian Travel Centre) but the railings were relocated in 1938 beside the grandstand in the Elphin Showground in eastern Launceston. In their new setting a cast-iron plaque was attached proclaiming that 'at Edinburgh in 1860 this fence was made of the first iron ore mined in Tasmania at Ilfracombe, West Tamar'. This might be modified to say 'the first iron ore mined in any quantity in Tasmania' to respect the earlier interest in Mount Vulcan, but the achievement is real enough and the railings are both extensive and handsome.

Not quite all the railings were re-erected, however. There was room for only 11 of the original 13 bays in the chosen site at the Showground and

The 1860s railings cast from Ilfracombe iron, in 1992 at Elphin Showground, Launceston. (R. Ian Jack)

only two of the three gates were reused. One partial bay was inserted clumsily nearby in the Olive Street fence, but the rest of the railings are no longer to be seen. None the less, the Showground railings, with their plain-worded plaque, are a striking memorial to the first stage of the process which led to large investments in the Tasmanian iron industry in the 1870s.

The iron smelted in Edinburgh therefore alerted people to the possibilities of native ore. Over a longer period, there had been an interest also in limestone. Throughout the nineteenth century there was an understandable preoccupation with finding iron ore in close proximity to smelting fuel, whether coal or wood, and to limestone as a necessary flux. The trinity of ore, fuel and flux was a constant concern at Mittagong, Lithgow, Lal Lal and Mount Jagged and was no less significant in Tasmania. The general commercial investor saw that a greater profit was likely from an iron deposit which incurred minimal transport expenses for fuel and limestone, so the immediate proximity of one or other, preferably both, was a selling point for company flotation until the twentieth century.

The search for lime in the early colonial period had been motivated by building needs, not by thoughts of iron-smelting. In Van Diemen's Land, as in New South Wales, the lime for mortar was initially supplied by burning shells, often from Aboriginal middens. On the Tamar, the beaches near Redbill Point were a major source of shells in the early years (and coincidentally one of the iron-smelters opened beside a beach there in the 1870s), but shell stocks were soon depleted and the need for limestone quarries was quickly recognized. By 1820 limestone deposits had been found just south of modern Beaconsfield and the stone was being burnt in a government lime-kiln. This spectacular stone structure with an unusual flared brick fire-hole still survives on private land beside the end of the Middle Arm of Port Dalrymple. It is an important testimony to the successful search for limestone ordered by the commandant of George Town in the Macquarie period as part and parcel of a building programme. Initially the limestone seems to have been quarried quite close to the kiln but over the next 30 years larger deposits of limestone were found and ultimately quarried further south, especially at Flowery Gully gorge some seven kilometres away from the early kiln. The Tamar Lime Works was established in 1835 halfway between Flowery Gully and the government lime-kiln, and this local industry was still healthily productive when business interest in iron ore finally became impelling in the 1870s.[11]

The catalyst in encouraging risk capital to develop an iron industry was, as so often, a geological report. In 1866 Charles Gould, the geological surveyor, reported to the Tasmanian House of Assembly on his extensive and intensive survey of the West Tamar iron deposits; political and business interest was immediately stimulated. Gould had spent some months around Anderson's Creek, inland from modern Beaconsfield, in the deposit which includes Mount Vulcan, and had dug trial trenches to test the depth and

Middle Arm lime-kiln, built of stone with a remarkable flared brick fire-hole before 1820. The fire-hole is seen from the north. (R. Ian Jack, 1992)

quality of the iron ore. His opinion was a professional confirmation of what Evans had published in 1822.

The major deposits at Anderson's Creek—up on Mount Scott and Mount Vulcan—were no more than 12 kilometres from the Tamar and its ocean. Although the Mounts were only some 100 metres high and were hardly iron mountains like the Erzberg at Eisenerz or, nearer home, Iron Knob or Mount Tom Price, they were, none the less, substantial and high-yielding ore bodies, separated from the coast only by flat country eminently suitable for horse tramways.

Excellent, proven sources of limestone were equally convenient, while there was an obvious potential for charcoal-burning in the uncleared woodlands. Suitable coal was lacking so, if charcoal proved unsuitable, coking coal would have to be brought in by sea. But the proximity to the shipping lanes made the importation of coking coal not unthinkable.

However, the translation of general interest into actual company formation and capital investment required more than a geologist's enthusiastic report. The sharp increase in the price of pig-iron imported from Britain in 1871 and 1872 supplied this impetus. With high price came scarcity, and for the first time a Tasmanian iron-smelting industry seemed likely to be profitable.[12] Tasmanian iron was particularly attractive to commercial men in Melbourne. Melbourne was not a city dominated by industrialization in the way that Manchester or Birmingham were, but in the 1870s, in the wake of gold-rushes, Victorian manufacturing became increasingly important and diverse. 'Unlike a pure industrial city producing a single main commodity for export, Melbourne's import-substituting industries generated a variety of subsidiary trades which further diversified and accelerated the city's growth.'[13] One of the common factors underlying all this diversity was iron: the nineteenth century was still the Age of Iron, and the sharply accentuated expense of importing pig-iron from overseas in the 1870s prompted the businessmen of Victoria to finance the 'import-substituting' smelting industry in Tasmania, just as it did a few years later at Lal Lal in Victoria itself.

In rapid succession, between September 1872 and January 1874, four separate companies were formed to smelt Tasmanian iron ore. The first, and best known, of these was the Tasmanian Charcoal Iron Company, which established a smelting plant near the mines in the vicinity of the new township of Leonardsburgh.[14] The succession of technologies considered is revealing: at first merely Catalan forges were mooted, but these were rejected in favour of a new process recently patented in Melbourne by W. H. Harrison using a wood-fired reverberatory furnace fitted with a retort which produced a current of hydrogen gas. The hydrogen then combined with the oxygen in the heated iron ore, 'liberating the metallic iron, which is left on the sole or hearth of the furnace in a spongy mass containing a little slag, which is

British and Tasmanian Charcoal Iron Company's plant at Redbill Point from seaward, showing the new jetty with rail track, the new blowing-engine-house and the blast-furnace beyond. The house to the extreme left is probably the manager's, which survives today. (*Illustrated Australian News*, 10 July 1876, p. 105; courtesy of Mitchell Library)

knocked out by an ordinary steam or tilt hammer'.[15] Harrison's furnace worked, and a small bloom was smelted and hammered into a single bar of iron on 20 April 1873, but the heat cracked the chimney stack and the works closed.[16] The company was re-formed in 1874 as the British and Tasmanian Charcoal Iron Company and the plant was totally reconstructed in 1875–6 on a new site, beside the wharf at Redbill Point.

This new stage in the company's operations is lavishly documented in the Tasmanian newspapers and vividly portrayed in lithographs published in the *Illustrated Australian News*, the *Illustrated Sydney News* and the *Australasian Sketcher*.[17] As a result of this documentation the technical and economic history of the British and Tasmanian Charcoal Iron Company between 1874 and its closure in 1877 has been extensively discussed in print.[18] The problems created by an irregular amount of chromium in the ore made the pig-iron hard to sell and a stockpile exceeding 4000 tonnes was unsold when the blast-furnace closed.[19]

Because the group of Melbourne businessmen who owned the Redbill Point furnace dismantled the plant systematically and sold it as building materials or scrap in 1878, little except foundations and detritus remained on the site after the 1880s. The iron casing of the blast-furnace was reused on the main line railway as three water-tanks, held aloft by columns from the elevator shaft,[20] but Western Junction (the nearest station) has had a concrete tank for many years and it seems unlikely that any of these examples of adaptive reuse of the furnace cladding have survived. The three Cornish boilers, the beam-engine in the blowing-house, the bank of 40 coke ovens to convert Bulli coal, the charcoal kilns for alternative fuel, the clay mill and the brick-fields have all gone, virtually without trace.

The footings of only one part of the plant are now visible and they will soon disappear beneath land-fill when an extension to the Redbill Point caravan park is constructed. The one surviving engine base is a brick and mortar rectangle 9 metres long, 45 metres from the shoreline. It is already partly obscured by fill but seven bolt-holes and one large iron bolt are still visible. The north-west/south-east alignment and its location suggest that this base supported the beam-engine, which is a central and dramatic feature of the 1875 view before the engine-house was built around it in the following year. Slag from the furnace was pushed over the bank on to the beach and the 3-metre-high mounds, partly disguised under white and yellow flowers, will soon be the only relics of the ironworks proper.

The jetty, as rebuilt in 1875–6, had its own importance, for it was the first in Tasmania to incorporate railway lines running right out to the deep-water anchorage, but there is no trace even of the piles. The line of the tramway, however, followed the present West Arm Road and can be confidently traced for 12 kilometres back to the quarries on Mount Vulcan. The location of the

All that survives of the engine-house and blast-furnace at Redbill Point is a single concrete foundation with a large wrought-iron bolt. Scale in 20-centimetre divisions. (R. Ian Jack, 1992)

Mining the outcrop of iron ore at Mount Vulcan in 1873. (*Illustrated Sydney News*, 27 September 1873, p. 9; courtesy of Mitchell Library)

jetty, itself fixed by the tramway, confirms the relationship of the surviving engine base with the beam-engine. On the other side of the jetty, a weatherboard house, 26 West Arm Road, is on the site of the ironworks manager's house shown on the very margin of an 1876 view, and is probably the original house somewhat modified.[21]

The iron quarries for the Redbill Point plant were opened first on Mount Vulcan in 1872 and were connected from quarry to plant by a wooden tramway. After 1875 the tramway was relaid with iron rails (and extended on to the jetty), but the same tramway route as in 1872 was followed, running due north from Mount Vulcan, turning north-east at the company town of Leonardsburgh and then curving east along the shore of West Arm to the company's plant.

The estimate of the remaining ore deposit at Mount Vulcan published in 1919 by Twelvetrees and Reid was less than 500 000 tonnes, with a similar amount available on Mount Scott just to the north.[22] BHP has recently taken an interest in the ore deposits but these tests have confirmed that mining would not be economic today. As a result of this lack of modern exploitation, the quarries used by all three Tamar companies in the 1870s are still largely intact though overgrown and in the bush, both near Anderson's Creek and at Ilfracombe.

A particular feature of the earliest of these iron-mines, on Mount Vulcan, is that W. H. Harrison, the innovative ironmaster at Redbill Point, employed dynamite there. Although nitroglycerine was imported in small quantities to Australia in the late 1860s, Nobel did not patent his invention here until 30

The main quarry in 1992, at most 3 metres deep, with drill-holes for dynamite and the mark '14'. Scale in 20-centimetre intervals. (R. Ian Jack)

The main quarry for ironstone on Mount Vulcan in 1873. The depth is exaggerated by the artist. (*Illustrated Sydney News*, 27 September 1873, p. 9; courtesy of Mitchell Library)

May 1872.[23] Harrison was employing dynamite at the Mount Vulcan mine within months of Nobel's Australian patent, using the name 'Giant Powder',[24] and the blast-holes are still very visible on the quarry walls today.

To test the Mount Vulcan deposit in 1872–3 a rectangular shaft was sunk at the south-west end, where the deposit is deeper. This was sunk to a depth of some three metres through ore: the quarry gradually absorbed the trial pit but today the bottom of the pit is still 130 centimetres deeper than the quarry floor. The quantity of easily extracted iron ore was still manifestly large when the smelting ventures all collapsed.

At Ilfracombe, the ironstone deposit at East Arm Creek was quite separate from the Anderson's Creek deposits which fed the other two smelters. It was not developed in so extensive a fashion, largely because of the much more rapid demise of the Ilfracombe blast-furnace. The surviving quarry is low-lying, just across East Arm Creek from the blast-furnace, and the floor is partly flooded. Two substantial piles of iron ore survive, one on either side of a rectangular loading bay, itself built of crudely shaped ironstone blocks arranged in five courses. This platform, 6 metres by 4.5 metres, presumably loaded directly on to a tramway or a wheelbarrow track crossing the creek on a trestle-bridge and then up to the materials depot near the charcoal kilns south of the furnace. The quality of the ore seemed excellent, with an analysis in 1872 showing 60.6 per cent of iron content.[25] When samples were smelted in the Melbourne foundry of Drysdale and Frazer in that year, the quality of the iron impressed the local commissioners for the international exhibition to be held in Austria, and a large bell cast from Ilfracombe iron was sent to Vienna in 1873. Other castings from the sample ore, such as cannon balls and a jaw for an ore-breaking machine, were retained in Victoria.[26]

The results of these test smeltings were widely known and scrutinized. In April 1874 the Albury newspaper, the *Border Post*, which was well informed about Melbourne affairs, reported the first smelting at Bogolong, a small New South Wales blast-furnace. The first Bogolong iron reached Albury en route to Melbourne on 2 April 1874: 'we are,' wrote the Albury journalist, 'only endorsing the opinion of several experienced persons in such matters, in saying that the pig is of an excellent quality, far superior to that of the Ilfracombe Iron Mine in Tasmania.'[27]

The construction of the plant at Ilfracombe lasted for most of 1873 and has aroused some confusion, but the combination of evidence from the two local newspapers, the *Cornwall Chronicle* and the *Launceston Examiner*, makes a coherent analysis possible. The usual optimism prevailed about making the new blast-furnace operable: in August 1873 the first tapping was expected by 1 September; on 5 September 'another month will see them ready for blowing in the furnace'.[28] In October confidence ran so high that a mould, made of lead letters with the Tasmanian crest set in a wooden frame, was manufactured,

The management of Ilfracombe blast-furnace, in expectation of their first smelt in October 1873, prepared this mould of lead letters set in wood to cast celebratory plaques. It could not be used, since the first tapping was delayed until November. (R. Ian Jack, 1992; courtesy of Queen Victoria Museum and Art Gallery, Launceston)

proudly proclaiming that 'this plate, one of six, was cast direct from first running of ore at the Ilfracombe Iron Company's works, Tasmania, October 1873'. The mould survives in the Queen Victoria Museum and Art Gallery in Launceston, but no cast plates are known to exist. And it is most unlikely that any were made because the blowing-equipment for the furnace blast proved to be defective and the problems were not resolved until late November 1873. The first tapping took place on 27 November and produced 2 tonnes of smelted iron, cast into 12 large pigs which were sent to Melbourne, 'a conspicuous landmark in the future history of this colony'.[29]

This much-postponed smelt, however, 'caused some damage to the furnace, and it was found that the blowing-power was not sufficient'.[30] Despite the substitution of two new and larger cylinders, when the furnace was blown in for the second time on 16 December 1873 the smelt failed and the furnace did not go into blast again.[31] Even the modest success of 27 November was questioned. In an editorial published a year later, on 9 December 1874, the *Cornwall Chronicle* made some indignant noises born of investigative journalism.

> It is just twelve months since we recorded the partial success of the Ilfracombe Iron Company, in smelting pig iron from the ore found on their property. We afterwards learnt, however, that this iron had not been fairly produced by any ordinary furnace process, and the subsequent collapse of the company showed this to be only too true. When attempts were made to produce the article in bulk from the large furnace, they utterly failed.[32]

The unfriendly reference to iron which 'had not been fairly produced by any furnace process' is opaque and ought not to be believed without question. The further development of the newspaper editor's argument is significant—despite the relative lack of success at the Derwent Iron Company's Hobart plant, and the alleged fraudulence at Ilfracombe, the future is none the less bright: the Tamar Hematite Iron Company is full of potential ('a new era will commence on the River Tamar and we shall soon see the whole Ilfracombe district bristling with life').[33] The *Cornwall Chronicle* editorial might be better judged by its silences. The only plant not mentioned is at Redbill Point, which was in the process of a dramatic reconstruction under a new and well-capitalized company registered in 1874: and T. C. Just, the owner of the *Cornwall Chronicle*, was a major shareholder in this new British and Tasmanian Charcoal Iron Company. The editorial of 9 December 1874 is a political statement and the Ilfracombe company was being made a whipping-boy for the slow beginning of the Tamar smelting industry in 1872–4.

Earlier in 1874, Just's newspaper had noted that Ilfracombe was in suspension, that Derwent had 'unaccountable delays' and that the Tasmanian Charcoal Iron Company at Redbill Point was still waiting for plant to arrive from Britain. 'We fear that in the colonies there are no men competent to undertake the practical manipulation of our rich ores, and we do not anticipate any satisfactory result until experience and labour of the right stamp can be imported.'[34]

The Ilfracombe company had, however, much better technical advice than Just allowed. A correspondent for the rival newspaper, the *Launceston Examiner*, commented in September 1873 that 'while another Company [Just's] has had each brick laid with a furious trumpeting the Ilfracombe Iron Company has gone to work steadily and quietly, but vigorously and determinedly'.[35] The detailed information supplied by this 'special reporter' who visited the plant after the furnace was completed but before the first smelting took place is the essential antidote to the *Cornwall Chronicle* and the essential document for the comprehension of the archaeological remains.

Captain Duncan Longden was the executive director among the ten shareholders in the Ilfracombe Iron Company, but the on-site manager was a civil engineer, Benjamin Hawkins Dodds, who had had experience in the Scottish iron industry. The team involved in the planning of the furnace was cosmopolitan. After the foundation stone was laid by the Melbourne merchant David Spence on 12 May 1873, the building of the furnace was entrusted to a Swedish furnaceman, Karl Haine, and the advice of James Baird Thorneycroft from Scotland was available. Thorneycroft was the son of a major iron manufacturer and the nephew of James Baird, one of the greatest of the Scottish ironmasters, who had between 1830 and his death in 1876 built up a coal and iron empire centred on Gartsherrie in Lanarkshire, with a large export trade to America.[36] When the furnace was assembled and ready for its initial pre-heating, it was James Thorneycroft who lit the first fire.[37]

The furnace at Ilfracombe still stands some three metres high in an open paddock bordered by bush, hills and two creeks. Its visual impact is powerful, far more powerful than Lal Lal, where the ruins may be grander but where regenerated bush and a cyclone fence allow no contextual vistas; and marginally more powerful than Bogolong standing 6 metres high on its picturesque terrace above Jugiong Creek.

The converse has happened to the Ilfracombe landscape: in 1873, 'through a dense forest, a clearing is suddenly come upon, and the works of the Ilfracombe Iron Company lie before'.[38] The comprehensive clearing on the flats has been achieved in the twentieth century in the interests of grazing, but already in 1873 there was felling which extended the ironworks clearing as a huge stockpile of wood was prepared for conversion to charcoal. The 2.4 hectares surrounding the furnace had been largely cleared between February and September 1873, producing 10 000 tonnes of wood. Some of this was used for building but the bulk was stockpiled.

The two charcoal kilns were remarkable. They were quite unlike the circular heap of carefully stacked and covered wood which is the most familiar style of charcoal manufacture: the heap was almost certainly in the style used by the Italian charcoal-burners at Lal Lal which was still being used in the Depression of the 1930s in outback New South Wales.[39] Instead the Ilfracombe kilns were a variety of the wood-charring ovens particularly associated with France but also used in America in the mid-nineteenth century. The French and American ovens were long rectangular brick structures bound with wood or iron stays at something like 1-metre intervals. The whole oven, which was fully enclosed and air-tight, might be as long as fourteen metres.[40]

Charcoal ovens used in France in the mid-nineteenth century of a style comparable to those at Ilfracombe in 1873 (though not so large). (F. Overman, *The Manufacture of Iron in all its Various Branches*, 3rd edn, 1854, p. 110, fig. 29)

At Ilfracombe the kiln walls were made of adobe, more than a metre thick at the base, tapering to 60 centimetres at the top. The size was extraordinary: 80 metres long, 6 metres wide and 3.7 metres high. Like the French ovens, the kilns at Ilfracombe were completely enclosed, with a woodwork casing to protect the mud-bricks from the weather. Furnaces lined with boiler-plate and faced with conventional bricks were built at each end of the kilns, with galvanized-iron flues projecting outwards. As in some French ovens, the Ilfracombe kilns could be opened at either end, which allowed 'the kiln to be opened for the discharge at one end while it is under fire or being filled at the other'. The reporter noted the economy of labour: 'These kilns, though so large, are easily managed, being completely under the control of the charcoal burner; and two men can by this means burn as much as fourteen could do under the old system [of heaps].'[41]

The two charcoal kilns were erected midway between the blast-furnace and the dam to the south: they must have left archaeological traces, but the area some 300 to 350 metres south of the furnace has not yet been explored. The important feature is, however, the originality of the concept in Australia.

Similarly, the blast-furnace was not entirely run-of-the-mill, while not being state-of-the-art either. The stone base with four arched recesses is still intact. This was a very standard design for the older style of furnace base and was still common in Haine's native Sweden.

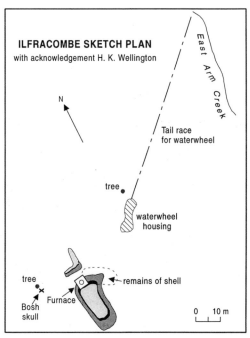

Plan of Ilfracombe blast-furnace site. (University of Sydney Cartography, with acknowledgement to Hugh Wellington)

Under the arches are the blast pipes in the form of a cross, from which they spring upwards to the tuyeres as in an ordinary blast furnace . . . These tuyeres are three in number, being situated one at each side and one at the back [i.e. north-west side] of the furnace, and are each fitted at the muzzle with a cast iron water chamber for cooling purposes, filled from a water cistern overhead, with which they are connected by a 1½ inch pipe. By an ingenious contrivance the water when heated again passes from the tuyeres into the cistern, and receive in lieu thereof cold water, so that there is a continual circulation kept up, and the tuyeres kept cool.

The tuyere pipes are still *in situ* in varying measure of completeness.

Above the masonry base is the hearth. What one sees now is the square setting of Garnkirk fire-stone, chosen for its proven lasting qualities in Scottish furnaces. Some Stourbridge fire-bricks were also used, as they were at Lal Lal, but the company, with its strong Scottish connections, chose Garnkirk for its strength and reliability. The contrast with the policy of the investors in Bogolong in New South Wales at the same time is striking. At Bogolong the fire-bricks were made locally on a country property called Woolgarlo: when the first tapping of iron was undertaken on 31 March 1874, the fire-bricks simply burst and had to be replaced by bricks from Sydney before the next tapping on 20 May.[42] Woolgarlo and Garnkirk were worlds apart in every sense.

At Ilfracombe between the Garnkirk hearth stones and the stone base is a solid bed of bluestone. Two horizontal air-flues ran under the hearth, each

Ilfracombe blast-furnace, north-east face, with all three tuyere pipes visible either within the recess or pointing upwards as goosenecks on either side. The long vertical bolt holding the furnace to the stone base is clearly visible to the left within the arched recess. (R. Ian Jack, 1992)

15 by 22.5 centimetres in rectangular section: other flues rose vertically from these through the upper walling of the furnace. The interior of the furnace, lined with Garnkirk fire-bricks, was 1.8 metres in diameter at the bosh, contracting to 90 centimetres at the mouth. Unlike Fitzroy, but like Lal Lal and Redbill Point, Ilfracombe had a tunnel head 3.3 metres high. An unusual feature at Ilfracombe was the decorated top. Around this tunnel head a gallery gave access to the firing-holes: unlike at Lal Lal and Redbill Point, the workmen on the Ilfracombe galley were protected from the weather by a conical zinc roof. 'This roof is painted in blue and white, and in addition to its usefulness is also ornamental, giving the structure, as viewed from a distance, a light and airy appearance.'[43] With a decorated top and blue and white cap, Ilfracombe was the gayest of Australia's furnaces. Still today its ruins, even without their blue and white zinc, are the most aesthetically pleasing of all ironworks remains in Australia, with the possible exception of the dourer Bogolong.

It was also functional. Unlike even the relatively state-of-the-art Redbill Point, Ilfracombe planned to reuse the furnace gases: provision was made for leading the hot gases off near the top of the furnace to heat the blast should the management decide to change from cold blast. Although the failure of the works to prosper prevented such developments, the provision is part and parcel of an operation which has been undervalued by posterity.

The simple comparison with Redbill Point has made Ilfracombe seem small and anachronistic. Ilfracombe was only 13 metres high against Redbill's 20 metres; it actually used only cold blast whereas Redbill Point used heated air from the outset; the fuel at Ilfracombe was charcoal, at Redbill Point increasingly coke; and the power source for the blast at Ilfracombe was planned to be a water-wheel, whereas Redbill Point had elaborate steam-engines. However, these contrasts are too sharp.

The attempted use of water-power was slightly surprising in the 1870s but it was both an acceptable technical option and the source of an additional archaeological dimension to the site. A substantial earthwork dam was erected 700 metres to the south of the furnace. The dam itself has been completely swept away by floodwaters but the channel which led the retained water round the dam in the direction of the flume is still a prominent feature. The second earth-dug channel just below the main channel and between it and the creek was a safety valve controlled by a log weir, 'being a provision for carrying off surplus water in time of a flood by a by-wash into the creek again' and also to control the regularity of the main flow. The flume was constructed of hardwood 60 centimetres across the base and ran for over 700 metres downhill to the furnace. Halfway, close to the charcoal kilns and the wood piles, the flume supplied water to a turbine, a horizontal wheel which drove the company's sawmill.

Ilfracombe blast-furnace from the south-east. The raised area is the sanded floor of the casting-shed. The single tree beside what is a flooded hollow to the right draws attention to the location of the housing for the 9-metre diameter water-wheel. (R. Ian Jack, 1992)

The tail-race from the sawmill returned to the main flume which led to the large water-wheel. It has been speculated that the wheel was never installed. It is true that it never worked effectively and that a steam-engine was used instead, but the eyewitness account of the site in September 1873 gives a detailed account of the wheel fully erected. It was one of the largest wheels in Tasmania, 9 metres in diameter, with 64 buckets made of kauri pine, 1.2 metres broad. The stringybark arms were sawn at Ilfracombe, but the iron stays and iron bosses were cast in Melbourne.

Although nothing visibly survives of the wheel, the wheel-housing pit is very evident still between the furnace and East Arm Creek. The waterlogged depression with a single small tree growing adjacent is 120 metres from the creek. There is no doubt about this attribution. The 1873 description describes the tail-race from the wheel as running underground through 'a tunnelled passage' to the creek '6 chains off': 6 chains is exactly 120 metres. The tail-race tunnel is now a slight depression in the cleared paddock. A previous owner of Ilfracombe partly filled in the depression with a large quantity of artefacts lying around the ironworks site:[44] the archaeological potential of this dumped material is quite high, although the research questions are very different from those on the furnace site or the sawmill site.

The heart of Ilfracombe is, however, the furnace itself. The remains have been recorded in recent years by Hugh Wellington of Launceston and by Don Reynolds of BHP in Wollongong.[45] Wellington completed his study in 1988 specifically to assist in the construction of the scale model now on display at the Grubb Shaft Museum in Beaconsfield. This model is extremely helpful for visitors to the site wishing to visualize the furnace in its heyday, but since the *Launceston Examiner*'s detailed description was not known to Mr Wellington or to the museum board, the model is deficient in a number of ways. The details of the top of the furnace could have been known only from the written account, and the relationship of the water-wheel to the furnace and its top-loading cannot be fully understood from the archaeological remains. The intelligent guess, realized in the model, that the top of the furnace was reached by a vertical, water-powered hoist is, unfortunately, wrong.

The materials for loading the furnace—ore, flux and charcoal—were in fact to be stored on a high platform, 12 or 13 metres high (much the same as the furnace), just to the east of the furnace (that is to say, between it and the water-wheel) and connected to the furnace by a bridge. The platform was already completed in September 1873 and the next stage was to build a storage shed upon it and a long inclined ramp on which the raw materials would be transported by a double tramway powered by the water-wheel. The materials dump was 110 metres away from the furnace, presumably near to the creek on the south-east: the surviving ironstone quarry is just across the creek to the east (though there are likely to have been quarries on the west side of the creek also) and the charcoal had to be brought from the kilns over 300 metres to the south. The ramp was to start at the materials dump and rise gently to the top of the platform 110 metres away. A turntable would be installed on the platform to turn the unloaded skip on to the down line. All this was ambitious and may not have been completed between September and December 1873; but the master plan was to erect a series of blast-furnaces which would be economically linked at the top loading level with the materials store atop the platform fed by the mechanized, water-driven tramtrack.[46]

The furnace base, 4.3 metres square, is faced with finely worked sandstone. This probably came from a small surviving quarry 500 metres to the north on the far side of East Arm Creek, near the manager's house.

The masonry work is fully professional and the sandstone has weathered well. The cold blast was introduced through passages 1.25 metres wide, arched with plastered brick three courses thick. The horizontal pipe within the lower furnace can be clearly seen in the arch, and the vertical goosenecks survive on the east and west sides. The patch attached to the western tuyere with screwed studs and nuts is at just the place where damage might have been suffered in November 1873 when the first attempt to tap the furnace went wrong, but it is more likely to cover a mundane manufacturing fault.

The tap hole was on the south side; although that part of the iron casing is now lying on the ground adjacent, the arrangement is clear, with a circular hole 34 centimetres in diameter. Moreover, a tap hole casting, with a hole 14 centimetres in diameter, was retrieved from the site some years ago and is now in the Grubb Shaft Museum at Beaconsfield. It shows no sign of use and has not been cast to fit the curve of the furnace shell, so in all probability was not installed. Although no trace of the tap hole casting which was used in 1873 has been found, its dimensions must have been very similar to the museum piece. Whatever casting was installed would have been particularly difficult to change, because of the way in which the furnace plates are riveted. Don Reynolds has suggested that the rectangular cut-outs in the loose plate containing the tap hole circle were an afterthought to make access possible; but since the cut-out section was not replaced by any removeable plate it is hard to see how this device could have functioned. The tap hole evidence remains ambiguous.

The furnace hearth was small and square. The removal of much of the iron shell has exposed the base of the hearth very instructively. Large horizontal slabs of fire-stone, imported from Garnkirk in Scotland, constitute the base, 84 centimetres square. On the south side this fire-stone base continues to the exterior of the circular furnace and indications of molten iron are visible close to the location of the original tap hole casting. Common bricks, some marked 'Cowen', filled in the remaining three semicircular gaps between the square hearth and the shell. The excellent condition of all these remains, while very helpful to the comprehension of the construction, is, of course, an unhappy commentary on Ilfracombe's failure to produce a signifi-

Ilfracombe blast-furnace, from the south, showing the hearth, 84 centimetres square, and the patch on the tuyere pipe on the left. The casting-floor in the foreground is overgrown and littered with brick and stone rubble. Amateur excavations have disturbed the area where the casting-floor meets the tapping area of the furnace. (R. Ian Jack, 1992)

cant amount of iron. The long, grassy mound running south from the tap hole was originally covered with a protective shed, 29 metres long by 9 metres across; it was built up level with the tap hole by its floor of sand, where the iron pigs would have been moulded if the furnace had ever worked on a regular basis. The whole site at Ilfracombe has an exceedingly high archaeological potential. Amateur excavation around the tap hole and the north end of the casting-floor area has demonstrated that much material evidence to assess the contemporary description is still intact below the present-day surface.

The archaeological potential of Redbill Point is now negligible; and the disturbances on the site of the third Tamar furnace do not suggest that a great deal remains under the surface or behind the brambles and the scrub. This is a pity, for the Tamar Hematite Iron Company was the most successful economically. It closed in 1876 not because of technical difficulties or collapse of markets but because of the death of the energetic manager, Algernon Swift. There were in fact two furnaces at Swift's site on the tidal part of Middle Arm. As well as the 12-metre-high furnace described by Morris-Nunn and Tassell, Swift built a much smaller furnace, also on a sandstone base, which he used to test the quality of the iron ore from Anderson's Creek early in December 1874. The editor of the *Cornwall Chronicle* approved heartily of Swift's caution:

> that gentleman, profiting by former failures, is anxious to make sure of everything before attempting to smelt on a large scale, and wisely practises in miniature. His small sandstone furnace is, however, said to be working admirably, and the iron turned out is of the very finest quality. Information received from competent authorities leads us to believe that Mr Swifte [*sic*] will be able to accomplish on a large scale what he has successfully done in a small way, and we sincerely hope we may be able to record the large furnace in full blast within a very short period.[47]

The large furnace lived up to the newspaper's expectations, was lit on 31 December 1874 and was tapped successfully on 2 January 1875.[48] Like Redbill Point, this furnace was built at the water's edge, with a jetty built out on to the tidal part of Middle Arm. Unlike Redbill Point and Ilfracombe, the furnace was built into a rock face and top-loading was a simple matter with the two charging doors accessible from a platform just beside the tramway loop.

This furnace at Swift's Jetty (now known as Scotchmans Point) was the most old-fashioned in appearance of the three Tamar plants. Like Ilfracombe, it was built on a square sandstone base, but its upper circular section was, like Fitzroy and Eskbank, clad in sandstone banded with iron hoops. Its height was very similar to Ilfracombe and the cold blast was powered by a similar steam-engine. Like Ilfracombe, it used charcoal and never coal.

The line of the tramway, the cart-road leading down to the casting house on the water's edge, some cut stone and iron supports in the face of the overgrown rock are all that survives of this small but quite successful enterprise. The three engine footings on the lower level appear to belong to a much more modern period, and the activities of the Golconda Gold Company have compromised the site. This company in recent years worked gold tailings, which leached from the nearby cyanide plant into the bay: the bay's hydraulics were altered by the construction of a limestone breakwater close to the site of Swift's vanished jetty and the silt has been systematically pumped. As a result, even the deposits of iron slag on the beach are exceedingly scanty compared to those on Redbill Point beach.

The three attempts at smelting local iron beside the Tamar have left remains in inverse proportion to the capital invested and the production achieved. Far and away the most ambitious and the most up-to-date technically (though still not thoroughly modern), the Redbill Point plant cost investors tens of thousands of pounds and has left heaps of slag, a beam-engine base and the manager's house; but these remains are essential elements in interpreting the various illustrations of the plant, which have a number of inconsistencies and show a varying degree of acquaintance with the site. Without the archaeology, the lithographs can be seriously misleading.

The modestly successful, trouble-free furnace at Swift's Jetty is quite well described in the local newspaper in 1874 and 1875, but a proper comprehension of the sensible system of tramway to the furnace head, dray-road to the beach and simple communication from casting-floor to adjacent deep-water jetty can be gained only from the site itself, however compromised and overgrown.

Despite the total failure at Ilfracombe, with its tiny amount of iron produced in two attempts 20 days apart, the site provides, along with Lal Lal and Bogolong, the most compellingly instructive survival of a mid-nineteenth-century-style blast-furnace in Australia.

The iron-mines which fed these furnaces were far from exhausted, since the furnaces were so short-lived. As a result the remains on Mount Vulcan and at Ilfracombe are, in different ways, interesting examples of surface quarrying. These quarries help in the interpretation of the destroyed iron-mines opposite the Fitzroy works in Mittagong as well as the Tamar Hematite Company's mine on York Town Road, while the old Mount Vulcan mine is strikingly similar to the cuttings with similar tramways at Lal Lal.

The human dimension to this promising industry which petered out within four years is still visible. The single miner's house still remaining in Leonardsburgh, the British and Tasmanian Charcoal Iron Company town close to Mount Vulcan, is evocative, though inscrutable: inscrutable because a second weatherboard house has been brought to within inches of the back of the original two-roomed house. Doors and windows were blocked as necessary and a four-roomed house with a back hall was created, perhaps for a miner's expanding family, perhaps for a farmer after the iron-mines closed and the company town became derelict.

The township around the company's smelting plant at Redbill Point called Port Lempriere grew up suddenly along Centre Street with 11 small wooden cottages shown on one side in an 1876 lithograph.[49] Only the manager's house on the opposite side of the street, attractively sited above the beach, survives in what is now West Arm Road, part of the Tamar Highway.

At Swift's Jetty, the Tamar Hematite Company built 40 workers' cottages as well as a manager's house but no surface remains at all are visible. Again Ilfracombe, despite the shortness of its life, reveals more about workers' housing. When the iron company took up this land in 1872, the half-dozen slab huts where the sawmillers had lived were presumably still there: they were described as 'dilapidated' in 1869.[50] But to build the furnace, to establish large charcoal kilns and to open up the iron-mine required more than sixty men at Ilfracombe by September 1873, increasing to a hundred by October. Many temporary huts must have been thrown up on the large estate around the blast-furnace half a kilometre south of the former sawmill. To the west of the furnace, some 300 metres distant, are the remains of two stone chimneys in the bush and, rather closer on the cleared paddock, disturbed ground and brick fragments mark the site of what locals describe as the iron company's bakery. At the manager's house, a discreet distance away to the north, there is a pleasing vista created by Captain Longden or B. H. Dodds around a house deliberately remote from the ironworkers' shapeless township. The manager's house stood between the two creeks, on elevated

The house built for the management at Ilfracombe late in 1873, now demolished. (Courtesy of Craig Sheehan)

The site of the manager's house at Ilfracombe in 1992, showing the two high hawthorn hedges at right angles to right and back. The pear tree in the left back is the main feature of the erstwhile garden. (R. Ian Jack)

flat land. Its extensive garden was bounded on two sides by water and on the other two sides by surviving hedges of imported hawthorns. To the visiting reporter in 1873 it was 'a pretty site enclosed by a remarkably fine quick hedge'.[51] In the garden one pear tree survives and another only recently died, while daffodils in the shadier parts emphasize the Britishness of it all, though the house itself with its sprawling inelegance and crudely thick verandah posts made of rendered brick was Australian vernacular of a rather curious sort. The manager's house, however, was quite clearly superior to the 50 wooden huts, just as the weatherboard house on the beach at Port Lempriere was distinguishable from the minimal cottages of the workmen nearby. The huts were built and furnished by the workers themselves on allotments provided to each man by the Ilfracombe management at 'a rent of 2s. 6d. a week if asked for it, which he is not unless he misbehaves himself'.[52] The stone chimneys in the bush represent these workmen's houses, the two or three stores and the bakery which flourished briefly.

Even in the material remains of housing, therefore, Ilfracombe is the most instructive of all the Tasmanian ironworks.[53] It is a classic case of the value of the total failure. The economic historians ignore it: Neville Wills does not mention it; Helen Hughes dismisses it in a garbled paragraph; and Damien Cash spends only ten lines on its history in his ANZAAS paper.[54] Archaeologists and historians of technology, by contrast, find Ilfracombe a marvellous site. Those who care about the cultural landscape indelibly marked by past industry can find here in Craig Sheehan's green paddocks, brawling creeks and tangled bush both a legible document and an aesthetic experience.

CHAPTER THREE

FROM GOLD TO IRON
IN VICTORIA:
THE LAL LAL FURNACE

The 1870s were characterized by feverish experimentation with smelting and processing Australian iron ores. In Tasmania and South Australia six companies were floated to smelt local ores, with a very modest degree of success; in New South Wales a new company took the moribund Fitzroy works and shook it into renewed production in the middle years of the decade.

Victorian businessmen had been the principal investors in the Tasmanian Charcoal Iron Company and its successor, the British and Tasmanian Charcoal Iron Company at Redbill Point in Tasmania, from 1872 until 1877. The Tasmanian venture was financed largely from Melbourne in the decade when Victorian manufacturing became really significant. At the same time the great gold-mining town of Ballarat embarked on an ambitious expansion of secondary manufacturing. The last 30 years of the nineteenth century saw the decline of the gold bonanza and the rise of the inland wheatfields of Victoria. The railway had joined Ballarat to the port of Geelong in 1862, and in the years from 1874 onwards Ballarat became the centre for a rail network extending north and north-west through Maryborough and Ararat. Weston Bate has summed up the result:

> [the railways] speared the developing wheatlands, securing for Ballarat an important share of the business of communities composed to a large extent of families who had previously farmed near, or followed trades in, the golden city . . . To the Pastoral and Agricultural Society's shows they brought a new mood, on the one hand warming the hearts of metal-workers with their enthusiasm for agricultural machines and on the other encouraging gentlemen farmers to breed draught horses to pull them.[1]

All this affected the metal trades greatly. Ballarat had a number of major foundries which had made fortunes from supplying the gold-mines in the 1850s and 1860s. Foundries like the Phoenix, the Union and the Victoria were obliged to lay off men in the late 1860s as mining orders melted away. The agricultural revival and the establishment of new mines far away from Ballarat gave the opportunity for more diversified sales in the 1870s. The Victorian government, moreover, under pressure from Ballarat notables, gave some protection to the foundries in 1871 by imposing a 20 per cent tariff on metal imports. In 1871 the *Ballarat Courier* was announcing to the world that, after the Phoenix Foundry had won lucrative new locomotive contracts, Ballarat was destined to be 'the Birmingham of Australasia'.[2] Just as Lithgow did not quite become the antipodean Pittsburgh, so Ballarat did not ever rival Birmingham. But the years in which these grand aspirations seemed realizable coincided with the rise in price and the reduction in supply of European pig-iron. The creation of a blast-furnace to process the iron deposits at Lal Lal close to Ballarat was an entirely natural development.

Lal Lal is 25 kilometres south-east of Ballarat. The township lies on the Geelong to Ballarat railway, opened in 1862. The area around the township is rich in workable minerals and clays: brown coal to the south-east, kaolin to the east-south-east, excellent clays to the west, iron 5 kilometres to the east, and some gold along the west branch of the Moorabool River and its tributaries.

The lust for gold was always a potent catalyst for other mineral discoveries. One gold prospector, John Skilbeck, set up a stamp battery to crush gold-

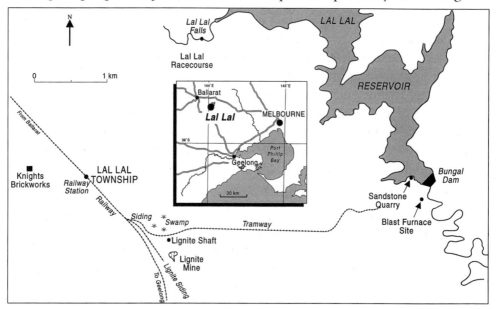

Location map of Lal Lal furnace in relation to the railway from Ballarat to Geelong, showing the tramway system which developed up to 1884. (University of Sydney Cartography)

bearing ore on the Moorabool in the mid or late 1850s; and from the future iron-mine site gold-diggings could 'be seen dotting distant slopes and gullies'.[3] These gold finds were, however, trivial in the context of the Ballarat field. Far more important for the future was the discovery in 1857 or 1858 of large deposits of lignite, a brown coal which has a relatively low carbon content, has a low heating value and was mainly used for steaming. The major deposits at Yallourn, east of Melbourne, have been of economic importance in the twentieth century for electricity generation and domestic briquettes.[4] At Lal Lal, more than sixty years before Yallourn was mined by open-cut, shafts were dug down to a 13-metre seam of brown coal at a depth of 21 metres and a 37-metre seam at 68 metres. The Victorian Lignite Company formed in 1863 consolidated work done there since 1857 and sent coal by train to Ballarat, Geelong and Melbourne. The brown coal was not very suitable as foundry fuel. James Bonwick commented in 1876 that although the Lal Lal lignite could be raised cheaply, 'some was very inferior stuff, not worth the digging. Light pieces shelled off in the air, and passed unburnt, often, up the chimney. Though other specimens blew well, the bars of the furnace soon choked up. Stokers did not like the lignite'.[5]

The brown coal was sold instead for use in bakers' ovens and used in steam-engines, particularly to drive the agricultural machinery in which some of the Ballarat foundries specialized. In the 1860s the lignite from Lal Lal was also mixed with water (it held over 40 per cent of water naturally in any case) and was made into briquettes, but it was never a major domestic product, unlike Yallourn's in more recent times.[6]

The lignite mines, extending south from Lal Lal township on the east side of the railway, encouraged population and gave the small settlement nearby a distinctively industrial character from the outset. This character

Site of Knight's brickworks near Lal Lal township. The flooded clay-pit is surrounded by brick fragments. (R. Ian Jack, 1992)

One of Knight's bricks beside the clay-pit, marked LAL LAL. (R. Ian Jack, 1992)

was confirmed by the opening of the Knight family brickworks just 1 kilo-metre due west of the township. Charles Knight dug the first clay-pit there in 1862, the year the railway line opened.[7] The quality of the bricks, includ-ing fire-bricks, produced by the Knight family from 1862 until 1898 was very high (as the 1875 school building at Lal Lal demonstrates today). The government geologist E. J. Dunn reported in 1910, 12 years after the brick-works closed, that 'the manufactured material was of excellent quality as shown by the fragments about the old furnaces. Besides fire bricks &c. a splendid hard blue brick could be manufactured at this spot. This is consid-ered one of the best firebrick deposits known in the State'.[8] The scatter of brick pieces around the deep, flooded clay-pit today is just as impressive in its evidence of quality as it was in 1910. The relevance of such a versatile brickworks to the encouragement of further industry is self-evident.

The date of the discovery of iron ore is uncertain. The year 1857 has been suggested, but this seems to be a confusion with the gold prospecting of John Skilbeck. The authoritative article on Lal Lal's brown coal published in *Dicker's Mining Journal* in June 1864 does not mention iron at all.[9] Some time thereafter, probably around 1870, the existence of substantial iron ore deposits was recognized and in May 1873 the Lal Lal Iron Company Ltd was formed with four shareholders: Andrew Knight, a member of the brick-making family, and three Ballarat businessmen. The company was formally registered on 18 February 1874 and its mineral lease over 320 acres (128 hectares) was granted two months later.[10]

The local businessmen, under the chairmanship of Charles Seal, were aware of the approximate size of the iron ore deposit and knew that its 50 per cent content of iron made smelting a potentially economic venture. Bonwick, who met some of the people concerned, gives a convincing account of the debate on the company board.

The main inquiry was whether the operations should be at the spot, or the [iron] stone removed. Though a sort of magnesian [dolomitic] limestone was near, the lime was inferior. The right stuff abounded near Geelong, the port, but that was forty miles by rail, and four miles more of a bush track. If the ore was taken to Geelong, where coal could be had from the ships coming direct from the Newcastle pits of New South Wales, the smelting could be readily done. The expense of carriage alarmed the directors. If they could have managed to smelt on the ground, that cartage [of ore] would be saved. Besides, the iron itself would find ready sale in Ballarat, where already [in 1876] steam-engines and locomotives are being constructed. To bring up lime from Geelong was not so formidable. As to the [Newcastle] coal, that would have to be given up. A vast forest covers the hills of our diggings' Country and might supply fuel for the works.[11]

So Geelong did not develop a smelting works and Lal Lal gained a blast-furnace.

The area containing iron ore was in heavily wooded country some ninety metres above the gorge of the west branch of the Moorabool. Because of the erosion of the side gullies on the west side of the Moorabool, the iron ore deposits were divided into several discrete areas. The principal area mined by open quarrying consisted of four outcrops within the 26.3 acres (10.5 hectares) identified by the government geologist, F. M. Krause, as containing over 700 000 tonnes of ore.[12]

In the 1870s only one of these deposits was opened, the one furthest from the blast-furnace: by 1877 several pits ranging in depth from 2 to 5 metres had been sunk and Krause reported gloomily in August 1877 that 'most of the limonite of commercial value for iron smelting has been removed and the remaining portion is too siliceous to be of much value'.[13]

Certainly a good deal of effort had gone into extracting iron between 1875 and 1877. It is said that Joseph Rowley, engaged by the Lal Lal Iron Company to develop the project, first tested the quality of the ore by digging a shaft on the steep slope with an access tunnel to the base of the shaft. 'Rowley then had the shaft filled with alternate layers of fuel, iron ore and limestone-flux, and after the smelting took the iron bars out through the tunnel.'[14]

This unorthodox experiment (if it really happened) was presumably successful, since Rowley immediately constructed the first Victorian blast-furnace in 1875, under the general supervision of E. H. L. Swifte, who had just returned from an exploratory trip to Britain. The first Lal Lal smelter has not survived, for it was on the same site as its 1880–1 successor. Speculation that the 1875 furnace was built some distance away[15] is categorically disproved by the admirable sketch-map which Krause appended to his 1877 report.[16]

The 1875 blast-furnace was distinctly minimal, both in size and in technology. The shell of an old boiler was set upright, lined with fire-bricks and set on a base enclosed in local sandstone. The fire-bricks were partly supplied locally, presumably by Knight—although Andrew Knight had sold his foundation stake in Lal Lal Iron Company in 1873 before it was registered, William, James and Charles Knight, all brick-makers, held shares from 1874 until 1876, the critical beginning years.[17] The really important fire-bricks for the hearth part of the furnace lining were, however, imported from Britain.[18] The furnace was only 9 metres high and the hearth was only 75 centimetres; whether 75 centimetres is the diameter of a round hearth or the side of a square hearth, it is smaller even than the furnace at Ilfracombe. Its 9-metre height was the same as Mount Jagged: among the 1870s furnaces, only Bogolong was lower.

There were close relations with the Lal Lal Lignite Company, whose railway siding was very attractive to the iron company, but the brown coal did not make suitable furnace fuel, although it was tried, either alone or with charcoal in the early years.[19]

The first blast-furnace at Lal Lal, erected in 1875, at its official opening in 1878. The pig-moulds are on the front left, pigs already made on the right. The furnace is simply an upended boiler, similar to the horizontal boiler behind. (*Illustrated Australian News*, 28 November 1878, p. 196; courtesy of State Library of NSW)

The first blast-furnace was fed entirely on charcoal burnt on the site. The Ballarat foundries had been using charcoal for years and, as in the United States of America, Italians had dominated this woodland industry. When James Bonwick visited Ballarat in 1876 he took a keen and sympathetic interest in the charcoal industry. 'It so happened,' Bonwick wrote, 'that the right men were handy for the purpose. For some years a few Italian immigrants had furnished the forges of Ballarat with charcoal. Some had been accustomed to that work at home, on the slopes of the Alps and Apennines. They had got into trouble with the Austrians in Lombardy, and avoided the dungeon by a flight to the colonial land of freedom.' Some of this group went to the Daylesford gold-rush, others turned to charcoal-burning.[20]

Descriptions of charcoal-burners (*carbonari*) are rare in Australia and little or no archaeological work has been done on charcoal-burning sites. Bonwick does not discuss the technology: but what he does uniquely is to place the Ballarat charcoal-burners in a vivid and realistic social context of prosperous isolation. These Italian men at Ballarat 'are first-rate workmen, being as steady as they are skilful. A party of four would rig up a bark hut; though preferring a living hut apart from the sleeping ones. The license to cut timber cost a pound a year, and the forest was enough for centuries. They knew better than our own people how to produce a good article, being patient and painstaking enough to burn the wood properly'. It was quite a vigorous industry: some *carbonari* could earn £5 a week, producing 200 bags of charcoal. This was for use initially in the Ballarat foundries and other manufactories. But by 1876 the part of the forest principally occupied by the Italians was near Lal Lal and in particular, as Bonwick relates, close to the iron-mine. One of the *carbonari*, James Plotzza, had a wife and children, and remained at Lal Lal in a cottage (built of Knight's bricks) as caretaker into the twentieth century.[21]

Since all this charcoal was manufactured by heaping the timber in carefully laid mounds, the archaeological trace is minimal. Even a high incidence of charcoal in the thin soil is often due to bush fires and the clearings confidently described by Staughton and Ashley (either with little growth because of the heat of the combustion a century ago or lush because of the nutrients in charcoal) are elusive.[22] Similarly at Ilfracombe, where large kilns were created by the charcoal-burners, no site has been definitely identified.

Suitable limestone was not available locally. Throughout the life of the two successive furnaces at Lal Lal, limestone had to come by rail from the Batesford area just west of Geelong and then (until the tramway was built in 1884) drawn by dray from Lal Lal railway station the remaining 5 kilometres to the furnace. But the iron ore was close and was easily brought down on skips by a short, though increasingly complicated, tramway system from the quarry to the smelter. Between the switching on of the cold blast in October 1875 and early 1876, pig-iron reported as either 110 or 125 tonnes was smelted from 230 tonnes of ore. This 50 per cent yield from the ore remained fairly consistent throughout the history of both furnaces at Lal Lal, during ten years of greatly increased capital investment following 1875.

After the successful smeltings in 1875–6 the furnace seems to have been closed for a time and an official opening was delayed until October 1878. Leading politicians and Ballarat businessmen attended the opening, and the Chief Secretary of Victoria was portrayed in the November issue of the *Illustrated Australian News* breaking the seal in the primitive furnace to fill 30 pig-moulds.[23] Production continued, but the output was too limited and in 1880 the decision was taken to dismantle the furnace and replace it with a better model. It is this furnace, built on the site of the old smelter in 1880–1, which survives so impressively today.

Ballarat interests in the controlling company (reorganized as a no-liability company in 1876) remained strong; and when this company was in turn superseded in July 1883 by the Lal Lal Iron Company the moving spirit was a local financial agent, William Little, several times mayor of Ballarat, and his fellow directors included H. H. King, the gold-rush ironmonger, and Cyrus Retallack, 'artist in wrought iron and doyen of Ballarat smiths'.[24]

When Little distributed his share advertisements for his proposed new company in June 1883, he could claim that 79 mine managers 'have had castings from the existing Lal Lal Iron Co.' The gold-mines included Ballarat stalwarts such as Egerton, Madame Berry, Black Hill, Buninyong and Loughlin's.[25] The geologist Baragwanath later commented that 'the quality of the iron produced was reported as very good but hard, and was used very largely for truck wheels and stamper shoes in the Ballarat mines'.[26] Ballarat was just as keenly interested in local iron in the early 1880s as it had been in the 1870s.

The second Lal Lal furnace was blown in on 26 March 1881 and over the next three years produced some 2260 tonnes of pig-iron: 560 tonnes (from 1092 tonnes of ore) in 1881, 300 tonnes in the first quarter of 1882, 600 tonnes (from 1200 tonnes of ore) in 1883, and in 1884, 800 tonnes (from 1600). The terminal closure in 1884 was due to the inability to compete with renewed cheap imports of pig-iron from Britain. The businessmen of Ballarat might invest in local industry but they bought the cheapest pig available and by 1884 that did not come from Lal Lal.[27]

The machinery on the site was all removed in the 1890s after an abortive auction sale and the stone cladding of the upper furnace was robbed at the same time, so that the photograph of the smelter taken in 1908 has an uncannily precise identity with the remains visible today. The site remains very legible, with the 18-metre-high furnace basically intact. The totality is the most impressive archaeological relic of the colonial industry in the country. Its preservation is due to its relative inaccessibility, to the wire fence

erected around it by Buninyong Shire Council in 1968 and to the protec-
tiveness of the Lal Lal Blast-furnace Reserve Committee of Management in
the 1970s, the Victorian Forests Commission and, today, the Department of
Conservation. The construction of access tracks by the Forests Commission
has enticed some picnickers, but Lal Lal Falls on another road some five kilometres to the north is much more popular with visitors today; while in the
past, Lal Lal Racecourse in the bend of Carey Road near the waterfall
directed most pleasure-seekers between 1874 and 1938 in the same northerly
direction.[28]

The other protection to the blast-furnace site has been Bungal Dam. This
large water catchment, backing up the west branch of the Moorabool to
form Lal Lal Reservoir, was completed in 1972. The dam and its pumping
station are within 300 metres of the furnace, but they lie to the north and
the main access road is from the eastern side of the dammed river. Part of the
original iron company's working area is now securely fenced off by the
Water Board, while the flooding north of the dam has covered only the footings of one of the bridges used by the ironworkers and their families to cross
to Bungal (which was closer than Lal Lal township).

The Lal Lal blast-furnace is unique among Australian blast-furnaces in
being built on an artificial terrace halfway up a gorge, with four more terraces cut out of the hillside above to accommodate all the ancillary engines,
structures and tramways common to such plants. The Fitzroy Company and
the Tamar Hematite Iron Company at Swift's Jetty had constructed their furnaces against a natural escarpment, which made for easy top-loading; the
others in Tasmania, South Australia and New South Wales were basically
planted on open paddocks and used either vertical hoists (at Redbill Point)
or inclined ramps (at Ilfracombe and Rutherford's Eskbank) to load the furnace. Only Bogolong was built on an artificial terrace, but it was a simple,
small-scale operation with no tramways or higher terraces, on a gentle slope
down to a smallish creek. At Lal Lal the furnace and the casting-shed were
on terrace 1; the furnace blast was generated by a large steam-engine supported on two massive stone pillars on terrace 2; and the smithy and carpenter's shop, a simple structure with light sapling walls, was on terrace 3 above.
On terrace 4 the main tramway ended at a large wooden shed where the raw
materials—charcoal (later coke), limestone and iron ore—could be stored
and wheeled directly to the top of the furnace along a wooden bridge
springing from terrace 4 and supported by three pairs of splayed logs on the
second and third levels.

Today, the furnace itself reveals all the important features of its construction. The base, as at Ilfracombe or Fitzroy, was made of local sandstone—the
fine quarry survives just above the water-level of the modern reservoir. The
stone facing was well worked, as elsewhere, and the tuyeres entered through

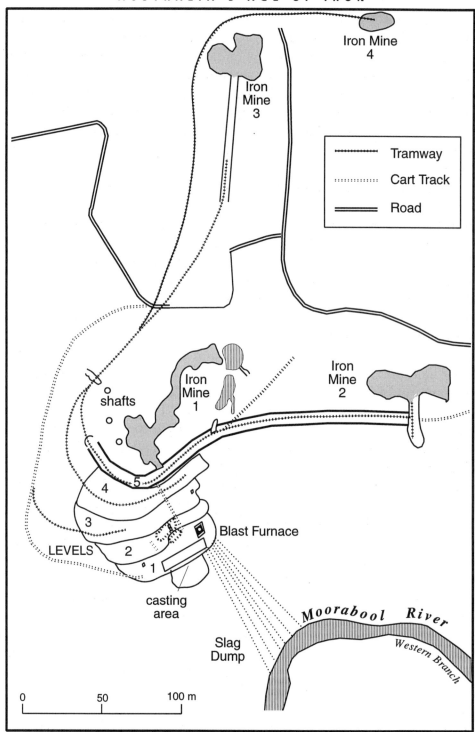

Plan of the Lal Lal furnace site, showing the proximity of the iron-mines, the local tramway system and the terraces on which the plant was erected. (University of Sydney Cartography, with acknowledgement to the plan on display at Lal Lal)

three handsome arches. On the fourth side, facing the river, the tap hole was also approached through an arched recess. The circular fire-brick lining, opening up to a diameter of 4.5 metres at the bosh and narrowing at the top to approximately two metres, was imported from Harris & Pearson of Stourbridge in England. The marked bricks, which can be inspected where the bosh lining is now exposed on the north-east face of the furnace, all show one or other of Harris & Pearson's stamps. In the earlier furnace on the site only the lower parts, the hearth and bosh, were lined with imported fire-bricks: the upper shaft used local fire-bricks, almost certainly Knight's.[29] The upper bricks have not been inspected in the 1880–1 furnace, so may also be Knight's, but Baragwanath's description of 1910 says categorically that 'the furnace was built of locally-quarried sandstone, lined with Stourbridge fire-brick'.[30]

The fire-brick lining was surrounded by a 5-centimetre layer of clay; beyond the clay, stone rubble filled the gap within the worked stone casing. The stonework above the lower furnace had four tapering sides consolidated by ten horizontal metal rods with vertical ties. The present appearance of the furnace, with the upper part of the stonework completely removed to reveal the tapering round brick shaft, is, of course, entirely misleading and we are

Lal Lal blast-furnace from the south. (R. Ian Jack, 1992)

69

A Harris & Pearson fire-brick, imported from Stourbridge in England, in the bosh of Lal Lal furnace. (R. Ian Jack, 1992)

Lal Lal: the clay packing between the interior fire-bricks and the sandstone cladding. The angle of the bosh is visible on this damaged north-east side of the furnace. (R. Ian Jack, 1992)

dependent on the 1882 photograph to know in detail what the furnace was like in its brief heyday. The shaft came to a flat, square top with a fenced walkway all round a 4-metre iron tunnel head, reached by the trestle-bridge, a very conventional design.

The furnace's cold blast was generated by a 50-horsepower two–cylinder engine with a 3-metre fly-wheel, whose turning circumference is still evident below the twin towers. The engine fitted into the rock-cut recess at the base of the east tower. On top of the two towers, bolts for securing the machinery are clearly visible from the terrace above; Staughton and Ashley in their report plausibly suggest that a rocking beam was installed at this level,[31] just as the British and Tasmanian Charcoal Iron Company had at Redbill Point. The steam-engine powered a pump to lift water from the river some seventy metres below just as an earlier, smaller engine had done in the 1870s.[32] The water was then distributed by an extensive piping system throughout the plant, but primarily to the two boilers adjacent to the blast-furnace on the first terrace. An underground flue ran from the boilers up through terraces 2, 3 and 4 to a metal chimney at the south end of the storage shed. This stone-lined and flag-covered flue (now partly exposed) and the well-constructed stone base of the chimney on level 4 are striking visual features of the site today.

Little of this is shown in the 1882 photograph, which was taken from the north-west: the engine and boilers were in any case within protective sheds. What is very clear in the photograph is the other function of the steam-engine.

The underground flue at Lal Lal, from the site of the boilers beside the furnace. The stone piers on level 2 to the left of the flue carried the blowing-machinery. The stone retaining walls at the back of levels 3 and 4 are prominent. (R. Ian Jack, 1992)

Lal Lal furnace in operation, viewed at the top level from the north-west in 1882. The furnace-top is reached by a trestle-bridge from the materials store on the extreme right. The carpenter's shop and smithy occupy the sapling-walled hut below the store. The building with the double pitched roof beyond the smithy is the engine-house, creating the blast which reaches the furnace through the large pipe at an angle, separating into three tuyeres. The very long building with a pitched roof below the furnace is the casting-shed and small foundry. (Department of Manufacturing and Industry Development, Victoria, Minerals Group Library, P622.09945 (942))

Lal Lal used cold blast, at a pressure of about fifteen pounds per square inch in nineteenth-century terms. From the engine a large iron pipe some two metres in diameter was angled downwards to the top of the south-west face of the lower furnace. There the pipe entered a junction box and horizontal small-diameter pipes led at bosh level round to the arches on the north-west and south-east faces. There the pipe went vertically downwards in front of the midpoint of the arch to enter the furnace, a characteristic gooseneck. The third tuyere, on the south-west side, was fed directly from the junction box. On the north-east side, the tap hole led to what must have been a curving channel into the long shed that protected the casting area. The slag was released to the north of the molten iron and poured straight down the steep slope above the Moorabool River, where it remains still.

The casting-shed's roof is visible in the 1882 photograph and its location is clear enough on the first terrace today. Its walls were substantial, hewn from the same sandstone quarry as the furnace. It was long, some forty-seven metres, because in the 1880s it fulfilled the dual purpose of producing pigs and doing on-site casting. A crane operated within the shed and in 1881 a cupola had been added to make a complete small foundry.[33] This foundry faced transport problems, just as the smelting operation did, since up to 1884 its products had to be carted to Lal Lal railway station. The company's strategy was to increase its involvement in foundry work and in 1883 it opened its own works in central Ballarat: the Lal Lal or Tubal Cain foundry at the corner of Urquhart Street and Lyons Street specialized in the manufacture of iron pipes, but did not long survive the closure of the smelter in 1884.[34]

The railway from Geelong to Ballarat passing through Lal Lal township had made the blast-furnace possible, since limestone had to be brought from Batesford and, as charcoal seemed less suitable for the 1880–1 furnace and the local brown coal was quite unsuitable, coke also came from the Geelong area. The lignite company had had a convenient railway siding since the 1860s: it is shown on the 1864 plan of Lal Lal township.[35] This initial siding had been extended in 1870, 1873 and 1875 and the final extension was used by a timber merchant. The iron company was allowed to use the lignite and timber sidings for loading and unloading but these sidings were all adjacent to the railway line and did not alleviate the basic problem of transportation

Tram line from the main railway to Lal Lal iron plant. This is the only known illustration of the tramway. The terminus must be just out of sight at the right back. The remaining 1.6 kilometres to the furnace could be crossed only by horse-dray. (Department of Manufacturing and Industry Development, Victoria, Minerals Group Library, P622. 09945 (945))

through the swampy bush to the furnace 5 kilometres away. The company had from the outset been aware of the desirability of its own tramway and had surveyed a possible line as early as 1874. Only in 1882, however, did it succeed in building its own platform and short siding beside the older lignite siding, and in 1883–4 it finally built a complete tramway. The route was level in its early stretches, the need for embanking was slight and it was completed in mid-January 1884. It operated partly by horse-traction, partly by gravity and can still be traced through cleared paddocks and the bush for most of its way.[36]

The railway historians have vividly reconstructed the ingenious working system on the company line:

> The siding on the government line was set in a cutting, and left the main line at a high point . . . When trains on the iron company's tramway were ready to depart, the chocks under the wheels would be removed, the brakes released and the horses would start to walk down the hill, around the curve to the south—a slight application of the brakes might be made here, as the curve was fairly sharp; then away they would move down the hill gathering momentum all the time, around the swamp, across the flat, then up one side of a small hill, down the other side and up another hill in lots 21 and 23, along the top and into the loop in lot 24; here if the line was clear the team [of four or six horses] would start off for the climb up the hill to the other loop on the top. At this point, if the line was still clear, the trucks, with brakesmen, were released to roll free down the hill to the works.[37]

For skips carrying iron from the mine to the siding, the procedure was reversed:

> Horses handled the load up the hill [above the furnace] to the passing loop on the highest point [on the 500-metre contour]; here they were taken off and if the line was clear the train would be allowed to roll down the hill through the loop in lot 24, down and up the next two hills where it would probably lose a bit of momentum, then down the hill to the curves and straights around the swamp (the brakeman would have slowed the train here) and on to stop at the company's siding on the railway.[38]

All this can still be explored today and it is clear that the high speeds reached by the skips (estimated at 100 kilometres an hour on the steepest incline in 1884)[39] must indeed have been exhilarating for the ironworkers and guests who sometimes rode the tramway.

The gap between the works end of the tramway and the furnace was 1.6 kilometres, and this had to be crossed by horse-drays. There was, however, another system of tramways, quite separate from this, which connected the iron-mines to the fourth and fifth terraces of the plant, beside the materials shed. The lay-out of this tramway system is clear in rough outline, although some of the details are more obscure than a plan can fully convey.

An iron quarry at Lal Lal, photographed in 1882. This is Iron Mine 2 on the plan (p. 68). (*Annual Report of the Secretary for Mines [Victoria] . . . for the year 1910*, after p. 66)

The original iron quarry of the 1870s, still the only one shown in Krause's 1877 map,[40] is the farthest from the furnace, about 600 metres away to the west. This is perversely marked as Iron Mine 3 on Inglis' drawing of 1971 and on Ashley's 1975 plan, which was published by Southern and Platt in 1986, but it is inappropriate to adopt any more rational numbering system now.[41] The original iron-mine is the most impressive of the four identifiable quarries. The long straight cutting for the tramway runs westwards into a partly flooded quarry with a face of ironstone 5 metres high on the east. A separate quarry (no. 4) to the north-west of the earliest mine is dug partly through an earlier tramway, with a loading platform at the south-east end. This quarry is not shown on the plans by Inglis or Ashley, but was probably linked to the tramway which ran past the south side of the earliest mine.

Much closer to the furnace there were two more mines. One of these, mine 1, was approached from the fifth terrace and, following the ore, developed a long meandering shape like a seahorse. Close to the north-east end of this, the largest (though not the deepest) of the quarries, there is a 'water hole' (as Inglis and Ashley describe it). This is in fact the dam of the 1870s shown on Krause's 1877 map, which supplied water by gravity to the engine-house below. The dam was supplementary to the successive pumps installed to lift water from the Moorabool. To the north of the dam was Iron Mine 2, a small clone of the earliest mine, with a short tramway running east–west through a cutting linking the quarry with a mullock heap on the breast of the eastern slope. An 1882 photograph of a mine which is probably no. 2 shows that the rail tracks were made of wood. Intersecting with that tramway is the main ore tramway running south on to the fifth terrace, past mine 1, and continuing in a massive loop round mine 1 to turn westwards in two forks, one to mine 3, the other probably turning north to mine 4. Another fork from this main ore tramway just south of mine 1 ran down in a loop east and north to end at the carpenter's shop and smithy on the fourth level. It is not known whether all the ore tramways had wooden rails, like the short stretch in mine 2. The tramway from the railway to near the plant certainly had metal rails, supplied second-hand rather grudgingly by the Victorian government in 1883–4.[42]

The furnace had been shut down in May 1883 after producing 600 tonnes of iron in four months; when the furnace was blown in again in January 1884 the rail link to the station had just been completed. During the next four months the highest production of iron that Lal Lal ever achieved (an average of 200 tonnes a month) was much more conveniently transported. In particular, the company's newly acquired foundry in Urquhart Street, Ballarat, became very active casting Lal Lal pig into pipes and mining equipment.[43]

But just as all seemed set fair for more regular and reliable production of pigs and their transportation to market, the price of imported iron fell sharply. Just as the abrupt rise in price in the early 1870s had been the essential prerequisite for the creation of the Australia-wide iron-smelting industry, so the plunge in the price of a tonne of imported cast-iron from around £10 to £4 10s in 1884 made Lal Lal uneconomic.[44] The cost of production of iron there in 1884 was around £5 a tonne. One hundred and sixty men were

The first iron quarry at Lal Lal in 1992, looking down the tramway entrance, from the east. (R. Ian Jack)

employed as miners, furnacemen, charcoal-burners, blacksmiths, carpenters, horse-handlers and tramway brakesmen, living in a motley collection of huts and houses in the area above the blast-furnace. Some of these men had families and their children went across the river to attend Bungal School.[45]

The whole infrastructure could not be supported once imported cast-iron was cheaper than the Lal Lal pig. So the blast-furnace closed permanently at the beginning of May 1884, the employees moved away, the houses decayed and today the bush has obscured all surface evidence of their very existence. Even the cottage made of Knight's brick and occupied into the twentieth century by a caretaker, the former charcoal-burner James Plotzza, and his wife, has vanished.[46]

The moveable industrial equipment too has gone. After an abortive attempt to reopen the iron-mines (but not the smelter) in 1889, the Lal Lal Iron Company's mining lease, machinery, tools and tramway easements were offered at public auction in July 1891. The auction was a disastrous failure: no one at all came to bid.[47] Presumably the equipment was then sold by private treaty and the heavy machinery was removed for reuse or scrap, while the stone cladding of the upper furnace was systematically removed, leaving only the lower furnace in its original splendour. All piping was removed, all the tramway rails were lifted and the site reverted to nature. The destruction of the industrial plant was complete by 1908 when two fine photographs of the blast-furnace were taken for the Department of Mines.[48] Since then, astonishingly little has changed: a single brick has fallen from the top of the furnace, but little more rubble has collapsed and the main structure is both evocative and legible.

CHAPTER FOUR

EXPERIMENT IN
SOUTH AUSTRALIA:
MOUNT JAGGED

Iron Knob and Iron Monarch, with their enormous and accessible cappings of iron ore, were not exploited until Broken Hill Proprietary Ltd took up leases in 1899 and carted the ore by bullock-dray to Port Augusta. From Port Augusta it was taken by barge across Spencer Gulf to Port Pirie and there used as flux for the complex smelting operations which isolated silver, lead and zinc from the Broken Hill ores.

Whyalla was created as a company port in 1903 and in 1915 the BHP smelters for iron at Newcastle opened. Thereafter the South Australian ore, increasingly from Iron Monarch as Iron Knob was worked out, was shipped along the Australian coast to be processed in Newcastle, the major rival to Lithgow and its successor, Port Kembla.

Finally in 1941 Whyalla had its own blast-furnace, with the coke coming from Newcastle in a reversal of the previous carrying trade.[1]

These places—Iron Knob, Iron Monarch, Whyalla—are part of the general Australian consciousness of South Australia's contribution to the iron industry. They lie outside the scope of this book. But they had a prehistory, which is an essential part of the general pig-iron crisis which afflicted the colonies in the 1870s.

There had been numerous discoveries of iron ore deposits in South Australia by 1870, stimulated by the better-known prospecting for copper and gold. When, in 1893, the government geologist, Henry Brown, published his *Catalogue of South Australian Minerals with the mines and other localities where found; and brief remarks on the mode of occurrence of some of the principal metals and ore*, he listed 17 separate iron ore deposits (including Iron Knob), 6 of which were already being used as flux in smelting other mineral ores.

The first smelting of iron ore took place in 1872 at the Phoenix Foundry in Gawler. James Martin, a Cornishman who had come to Australia in 1847, started a blacksmith's business in Gawler the following year and expanded it into a major engineering works and foundry in the 1850s. This Phoenix Foundry was manufacturing large castings from imported pig or scrap-iron, culminating in the Virginia bridge girders in 1868. Martin saw the possibility and desirability of using local ores and in 1872 constructed a small charcoal-fuelled smelter in his foundry to treat ore from the Barossa. The local newspaper, the *Bunyip*, reported that on 8 November 1872 their journalist visited the Phoenix Foundry just after the smelting 'and had the satisfaction of seeing turned out of the moulds, of excellent quality, cog wheels, ploughshares, a medallion portrait, looking glass frame, handsome picture frame, and various other articles, including a tea cup with saucer and teaspoon'. With the usual optimism, the journalist concluded that

> the fact is thus established that we shall be able to rear up and multiply metallic pigs to any extent. Messrs. M[artin] & Co. are now constructing the necessary appliances for a movement on an enlarged scale, Barossa supplying both the iron ore and the charcoal, and we need hardly say that the realization of this great desideratum must prove of vast importance ... [2]

Though Martin did not persevere with smelting Barossa iron, at least one very public memorial to his initiative still stands in Murray Street, Gawler's main thoroughfare. The iron railings outside the Gawler Institute, of which Martin had been a founding member in 1870, have a central pillar cast at the Phoenix Foundry in 1879, bearing the inscription 'Cast from the first iron smelted in the colony at the Phoenix Foundry 1871 from ore raised in the district of Barossa / Presented by James Martin Esqr J.P. / 1879'.

Martin's memory deceived him and the correct date is 1872 not 1871, yet another salutary caution about the dependability of evidence. In the Gawler case, the evidence of the *Bunyip* is precise and contemporary while the Institute plaque was cast some seven years on. (At Ilfracombe in Tasmania the moulding pattern giving the date October 1873 for the first smelt is similarly misleading.) Material evidence has primacy only when it deserves primacy.

The Gawler railings consist of only two bays divided by the column cast with Martin's inscription. There is no gate—the stone-flagged verandah behind is open at both sides. Altogether this is a modest monument to the beginnings of South Australian iron ore smelting, lacking the exceptional qualities and size of the Launceston railings cast in Edinburgh in 1860 from Tamar ore; but, unlike the Tasmanian iron, this was at least smelted in its colony of origin.

Martin's successes late in 1872 were no doubt known further afield. His example, coupled with the rapid rise in price of imported pig-iron, encouraged the formation of the South Australian Iron and Steel Company in

CAST FROM THE FIRST IRON SMELTED IN THE COLONY AT THE PHŒNIX FOUNDRY 1871 FROM ORE RAISED IN THE DISTRICT OF BAROSSA

Gawler Institute, Gawler, 1879 plaque commemorating the smelting of Barossa iron ore in 1871 (in fact in 1872). (R. Ian Jack, 1992)

1873. The prime movers were local businessmen Sidney Clark, son of the owner of a major foundry at Port Adelaide, and C. L. Dubois, who became manager of the blast-furnace.[3]

The ore deposit for the new venture lay to the south of Adelaide, near the top of Mount Cone on the Fleurieu Peninsula. It lay some three kilometres north of the Myponga to Victor Harbor road and the ore was brought down a track with many corduroy sections, using split logs to make a passable surface for the horse-drawn wagons. Despite the location on what is now known as Mount Cone, the name 'Mount Jagged' was consistently applied to this iron-mine. Mount Jagged, as at present defined, is 5 kilometres east of Mount Cone and the old terminology, using 'Mount Jagged' for a whole section of the South Mount Lofty Ranges, has created confusion. This confusion is not helped by the difficulty of describing the location of the blast-furnace built in 1873 by the South Australian Iron and Steel Company. It is convenient, and conventional, to call it the Mount Jagged furnace, but the furnace is 5.5 kilometres south-west of Mount Jagged and 4 kilometres south-east of the iron-mine on Mount Cone as the crow flies. In fact the wagons had to travel about nine kilometres from quarry to furnace.

The furnace was erected close to the Hindmarsh River, at its junction with an unnamed tributary. The furnace was minimal in height (a mere 9 metres) and old-fashioned in design, using cold blast and charcoal, like Ilfracombe or Swift's Jetty in Tasmania. There are no remains of the furnace itself and Dubois' own description is rather general: 'smelting works, consisting of a furnace 30 feet high, engine and blowing cylinder, and the necessary sheds, were erected, at a cost of about £2500.'[4]

A long account of the short life of the blast-furnace was supplied by Dubois to the *Illustrated Adelaide News* and published in January 1875. The furnace was blown in on 28 July 1874 and produced a little iron:

> Having completed alterations and repairs I filled the furnace again on 7th September and commenced charging on the 8th. Worked to the 10th when a mass of half fused iron and slag had collected in the hearth and the furnace-keepers having quarrelled, each one accusing the other of incapacity and neglect, I was obliged to take off the wind and draw the charge, about 3 tons of iron of variable quality having been made.

Dubois again repaired the furnace and coaxed it into smelting from 18 to 26 September, but the accumulation of iron and slag in the base of the bosh became critical again. Dubois blamed the problem on moisture entering the

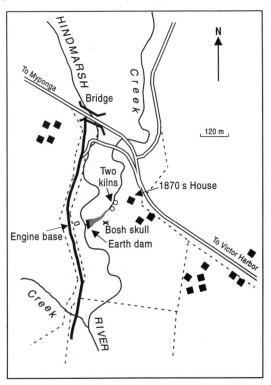

Plan of blast-furnace site near Mount Jagged. (University of Sydney Cartography, based on plan by Peter Bell and R. Ian Jack)

furnace hearth through 'the damp earth and brickwork round the furnace'. He cleaned the hearth out again and turned on the blast on 19 October. But the tuyeres were obstructed and the furnace could not draw at all, so again repairs were made. The furnace was relit on 28 October but 'finding the furnace work just as bad I had to stop again on the 30th'.

The South Australian Iron and Steel Company was then taken over by the Port Adelaide foundry firm of Francis Clark, father of Sidney. Dubois remained as manager; he reread his textbook, Hilary Bauerman's *A Treatise on the Metallurgy of Iron*,[5] made adjustments and the furnace went into blast again on 28 November 1874. But, although Dubois had finally eradicated the 'obstructions', the furnace had not recovered from all its earlier vicissitudes and 'cracked and opened in every direction round the bottom'. So the Mount Jagged smelter closed down on 5 December 1874 and did not reopen.[6]

Dubois' very detailed and apparently frank explanations of the furnace's performance give a context to the inscrutable remains. On the south side of the Myponga to Victor Harbor road there is a farmhouse, built largely of stone rubble. The house is consistent with a date in the 1870s and may have been the accommodation used by Dubois when he was manager. In its back garden there are pieces of slag and some refractory bricks, as well as miscellaneous metal objects.

The paddock south of the farmhouse varies from being damp to being a mud-bath. On the west there is an unnamed creek running south into the Hindmarsh River which cuts across the south edge of the paddock. This unnamed creek is dammed by a substantial earthworks close to its confluence

Stone rubble farmhouse of 1870s on Mount Jagged blast-furnace portion, probably the home of Dubois, the manager, in 1874, showing the south-west side of the back of the house. (R. Ian Jack, 1992)

with the Hindmarsh. The creek runs through a gap on the east side of the earth dam, so the dam is impossible to approach save by crossing the swollen creek or by crossing the Hindmarsh River from the south or west. There is still today, after 120 years of presumed neglect, a substantial pond immediately north of the dam, and when the outlet was narrower it would have backed up rather further. Dug into the shelving east bank of the creek, about 80 metres from the farmhouse and 120 metres north of the dam, are two depressions resembling kilns. They are completely grassed over but there are unmistakable signs of a masonry or brick structure consisting of at least two parallel walls enclosing a pit dug into the bank. At first it seemed plausible that both were lime-kilns. Some lumps of crystalline limestone are visible close to the structures, and in 1887 Dubois had commented that the limestone deposit 'was in huge boulders, and of so hard a character that lithofracteur [dynamite] had to be used in working it'.[7] It is likely that prior burning of so intransigent a limestone, before its use as flux in the furnace, would have recommended itself to the management. Certainly at Fitzroy in New South Wales a decision was taken in 1865 'to burn the limestone before putting it into the Furnace whereby a great saving would be effected'.[8] At Ilfracombe the remains of a very small lime-kiln are built into the bank of the creek near the blast-furnace in a way analogous to the Mount Jagged plant; it is, however, likely that the lime burnt at Ilfracombe was used in the building of the miners' houses and the industrial structures rather than in the charging of the furnace itself.

Mount Jagged: the blast-furnace site from south-west. The Hindmarsh River runs across the middle of the photograph, below the rectangular concrete engine base. The dam across the tributary creek is just beyond the Hindmarsh. The bosh skull (not visible) lies in the paddock to the right, beyond the river, the two kilns on the east bank of the creek and the farmhouse/manager's house is in the centre back. (R. Ian Jack, 1992)

One of two calcining kilns, perhaps for iron ore, perhaps for lime, to the east of the creek at the Mount Jagged ironworks site, taken from the north-west. (R. Ian Jack, 1992)

There is a balance of probability that at least one of the two kiln-remains at Mount Jagged was used for burning lime. It is hard to see why two substantial lime-kilns, 7 metres apart, would be necessary. An attractive explanation for the second kiln is that it was used for calcining the iron ore before it was fed into the furnace. This was a well-known procedure in nineteenth-century iron-making.

Many kinds of ore [wrote Alder Wright in 1880] are unsuitable for use in the blast furnace without some preliminary treatment,—consisting either of washing with water and dressing in the ordinary way adopted with heavy minerals to wash out clay, &c; weathering by exposure to oxidize pyrites, &c., and wash out the soluble matters formed; roasting, so as to expel carbon dioxide and water and burn off organic matter, peroxidizing the iron in so doing; or a combination of some or all of those processes.[9]

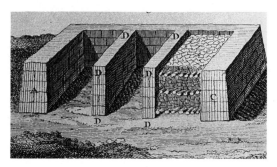

Ore-calcining kiln in eighteenth-century Sweden, similar to apparent construction at Mount Jagged. (Diderot, *Recueil des Planches*, 5me livraison, vol. 6, 1768, Minéralogie, Calcination des Mines, plate 1, fig. 3)

Brown hematite ore at Fitzroy in the 1860s was roasted to eliminate the surplus water content, and to volatilize other extraneous matter. A simple open-air method was used, without any kiln structure, and the ore was 'burnt on huge stacks of wood and coal, something after the same manner as you will see shells burnt for lime'.[10] The calcining pile is clearly visible just beside the road in a photograph of this time. Although the Fitzroy board, under Ebenezer Vickery, had queried the necessity for such calcining in 1868,[11] the practice was still being followed in 1876 under David Lawson's management; at this time some veins of the iron ore in the mine just across the southern road from the Fitzroy works, were 'smelted without being calcined, but by far the larger portion has to undergo this operation'.[12] An open heap is unsophisticated. The practice of digging a pit for calcining iron ore is a halfway house between the pile and the high enclosed kiln which became common in Europe in the nineteenth century, and which was used in Australia to calcine auriferous quartz at Maldon and Hill End.[13] The humbler roasting pit is documented archaeologically in Sweden and Ivar Bohm has described how a pit was dug into the slope of a hill, as at Mount Jagged. In Sweden 'where the terrain offered no protection, a wall of granite was constructed and two side walls. Wood and ore were stacked in layers and ignited in the roasting pits or stalls'.[14] The overgrown remains at Mount Jagged may very well reveal such an ore-calcining pit if excavated: as a hypothesis, the existence of one simple lime-kiln and one ore-roasting pit is attractive.

The reason for roasting the Mount Jagged ore, if roasted it was, may have been an attempt to counteract the difficulty of the ore which contained a

Bosh skull at Mount Jagged, in context, with scale marked in 20-centimetre intervals, taken from the north-west. The fire-bricks adhering to the skull are visible on the right-hand side. (R. Ian Jack, 1992)

worrying amount of titanium. This may not have been known to Dubois; the geological report of 1915 which analysed some of the ore left stacked in the open-cut mine in 1874 is the first to publish its full composition and to draw attention to the American experience that 'under present furnace practices . . . the smelting of these ores [containing around 3 per cent of titanium] is both difficult and expensive, and for that reason they are not accepted by furnaces'.[15]

This difficult ore was, however, smelted with some success at Mount Jagged and 50 metres away to the south-west of the two roasting-pits/kilns is a bosh skull. This lies in a circular depression in the lush paddock and may be the iron and slag left behind when the furnace was demolished. Alternatively, it may be part of the material removed from the furnace hearth on those three occasions in September and October 1874 when the hapless Dubois was obliged to turn off the blast.

The skull is an irregular circular shape, with a minimum diameter of 88 centimetres, a maximum of 108. Some twelve centimetres of smelted iron lie on the top and twenty-seven centimetres of slag and other rubbish below as it is currently positioned. The similar skull at Ilfracombe has maximum dimensions of 40 by 30 centimetres but this is not an adequate guide to the respective dimensions of the furnaces. Both skulls are too heavy to move and cannot be examined comprehensively. The Ilfracombe skull came from a furnace whose dimensions are known: the hearth is intact and measures 84 cen-

Bosh skull, from the north-east, showing the flat layer of smelted iron on top and the slag mixture below. Scale in 20-centimetre intervals. (R. Ian Jack, 1992)

timetres square. The Mount Jagged skull is the only indicator of the furnace's dimensions, since only the height, a modest 9 metres (4 metres less than Ilfracombe), is given in the documentary accounts.

Still adhering to one side of the skull are eight red fire-bricks. These are flared, to form the circle of the furnace well, measuring 11 centimetres on the outer side and 7 centimetres where they join the slag and iron. The refractory brick fragments lying around in the depression are yellow, together with some red common bricks. The origin of the fire-bricks is not known, although it is most unlikely to have been local.

The skull lies in the centre of a depression consistent with the foundations of a small blast-furnace and its engine-house, but an excavation of the site would be the only way to clarify the uncertainties. This is the only colonial blast-furnace in South Australia to have operated outside Martin's Gawler foundry (and only a façade remains of that great building); a small controlled excavation would therefore be appropriate.

An excavation is doubly necessary, because there is an unexpected concrete engine base across the Hindmarsh River to the south, opposite the confluence with its tributary. The river is inconveniently deep for easy crossing; the road from the iron-mine to the farmhouse and the lime-kilns had already bridged the Hindmarsh just to the west; and the track to the concrete base is merely an access road to a property called Cressbrook. But the base is made of concrete with embedded pebbles and shells consistent with

Concrete engine base with wrought-iron bolts beside the Hindmarsh River, with an apparent terrace running south-east between the base and the tree. The human scale is provided by Peter Bell. (R. Ian Jack, 1992)

the Fleurieu Peninsula shoreline and with a nineteenth-century date; it is elevated above the river on what seems to be an artificially formed terrace running for some one hundred metres to the south. Four large wrought-iron bolts still protrude from the engine base and it is difficult to dissociate it from the iron-working operation. It looks just like a base for a blowing-engine. However, because of the consistency of the remains on the other side of the river—the house, the slag, the skull, the kilns—it is difficult to accept that the blast-furnace was in fact beside this engine base. Even with a trestle-bridge across the river (of which there is no trace), the arrangement is clumsy and unnecessary. But none of us who have seen the site has been able to produce any adequate explanation for the engine base.

Whatever stood on the base, it is unlikely to have been used after 1874. Hopes for the iron industry did not immediately die. In 1876 J. B. Austin blamed high labour prices and the shortage of suitable coal deposits for the failure to exploit the ores already discovered. He drew attention to the purity of some outcrops: 'Native iron has been found so pure that it has, without any preparation, been welded on to a piece of manufactured iron, and stood well.' As for Mount Jagged, Austin described the 'production of first-class pig iron, and its subsequent manufacture into wrought iron and steel' as 'highly successful'.[16] But a Goolwa foundryman, called Graham, who was a share-holder in the iron and steel company, and had used 5 tonnes of Mount Jagged pig, had already complained that unless it could be made 'softer' it would not be suitable for general foundry casting.[17] Although he did not know it, Graham was bemoaning the presence of titanium. It is not surprising that, as Austin commented, 'the shareholders in the company . . . lost heart, and the [Mount Jagged] project was for a time abandoned. Several of those who first took the matter up, however, have still great faith in the ultimate success of iron smelting in South Australia, and as our population increases, and other favourable circumstances arise, we may expect to see this important industry revived'.[18]

Revived it was, but 67 years elapsed between the closure of Mount Jagged and the opening of Whyalla.

CHAPTER FIVE

THE FORGOTTEN
FURNACE: BOGOLONG,
NEW SOUTH WALES

The Great Southern Road passes through rolling upland country west of Yass. At Bookham, the quiet road north to Illalong and Binalong follows the well-wooded course of Jugiong Creek. An older road meanders gently to the west, connecting the early pastoral stations of Bogolong, Mylora and Illalong. It is the quintessential southern tableland, with fine-wooled sheep still dotting the hillsides even in a pastoral recession. There are only two surprises: one, the herd of pedigree zebus, is mild; the other is abrupt and exciting. The road passes through quite high banks, but about three kilometres from Bookham the top of a stone tower catches the eye beyond the paddock fencing to the west. There are concrete storage silos in the district of similar dimensions, but the stone tower is part of the only surviving colonial blast-furnace in New South Wales. From the top of the bank the vista over the sweeping bends of the creek encompasses the whole of Bogolong ironworks: trim, self-contained, close to all its raw materials and retaining intact its external appearance of 1874.

This satisfying industrial monument is the least known of all Australia's ironworks of the 1870s. Southern and Platt quoted a single newspaper report about Bogolong in their survey of Australian iron-making before 1914,[1] but made no comment and did not pursue the remark of the geologist Jaquet in 1901 that 'the remains of the furnace are still standing'.[2] No picture, no description, of the furnace has ever been published, and it is not well known even to the people of Bookham.

The Bogolong Iron Mining Company, which sought registration in 1873, had an initial capital of £1200 supplied partly by two local Bookham men (Robert Stracey and George Rees), partly by four Albury investors (Richard Thomas Blackwell, Andrew Edward Heath, Thomas Affleck and John

Bogolong blast-furnace from the south-east, showing the casting-floor terrace in front and the rock-cutting at the back. (R. Ian Jack, 1993)

Charles Gray). The manager (also a shareholder) was Thomas Blackwell, from the Victorian mining area of Daylesford.[3] Certainly the manager and Riverina investors were familiar with the Melbourne scene and with the Victorian investment in the Tamar Valley ironworks of Tasmania. The local Albury newspaper in March 1874 drew attention to an overseas journal, the *English Mechanic and World of Science*. This influential journal had published an article entitled 'Iron manufacture in the colonies', based on a letter from a Sydney correspondent printed in the *Wolverhampton Chronicle*. 'We are told, upon what appears to be reliable authority, that within the last few months discoveries have been made in New South Wales which will shortly enable that colony to supply iron of superior quality cheaper than any other part of the world.' All this happening in Australia in 1873–4, the *English Mechanic* considered, 'may be the commencement of such a revolution in the iron trade as may entirely change the circumstances of [South Staffordshire] with its worked out collieries and its numerous trade disputes'.[4]

The letter from Sydney had referred to the good prospects at Wallerawang, near Lithgow, but might equally have referred to Bogolong. Since July 1873 seven workmen had been mining the iron ore deposits and building a smelting plant. The ore was hematite 'of excellent quality'[5] and was thought to be readily available over much of the 80-hectare lease taken by the Albury group of investors. The real extent of the ironstone remains unknown, and what Jaquet said in 1901 still holds true: 'the deposit is probably of considerable

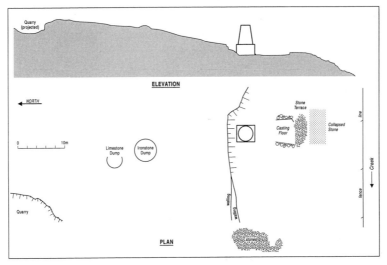

Plan of Bogolong blast-furnace. The tap hole of the furnace is on the south side, with the pig-beds on an artificial terrace built up by a stone wall, overlooking Jugiong Creek. The north face of the furnace is close to the rock-cutting, which defines the end of the casting-terrace and the exit road curving north-eastwards towards the Bookham–Illalong road. Above the furnace to the north-west is the probable site of the blowing-engine for cold blast. Twenty metres to the north are stockpiles of ironstone and limestone and west of these is the ironstone quarry which extends to the top of the hill. (A. Cremin and University of Sydney Cartography)

extent, but its dimensions cannot be correctly ascertained on account of the bed-rock in the vicinity being hidden from view by alluvium.'[6] The quality of the ore is clear enough, however, and a nineteenth-century analysis showed that it contained 52 per cent metallic iron, less than the 70 to 80 per cent yield confidently forecast in 1874, but reasonably economic.[7]

The proximity of the ore deposit to the creek, to limestone and to heavy timber for charcoal-burning inspired understandable optimism in 1873 and 1874. The siting of the blast-furnace was thoughtful and sensible. The part of the iron deposit which was opened up in 1873 lay on the edge of the flat above what is now called Jugiong Creek but which in the nineteenth century was known as Bogolong Creek. The land fell away to the south to the wide and sandy creek 100 metres distant. A stockpile of ironstone was established 20 metres below the edge of the mine, a similar stockpile of limestone lay closer to the mine and presumably charcoal was burnt in heaps somewhere not far away. The limestone quarry has not been located but the whole Bookham area was known for its 'very rich limestone'.[8]

From the ironstone stockpile a trestle-bridge 20 metres long was almost certainly constructed to lead to the open top of the furnace. The furnace stood 6 metres high halfway down the slope to the creek, erected on an artificially developed terrace supported by a stone retaining wall. The hillside was cut back so that the furnace sat snugly in a sheltered site, with optimum loading convenience. In front of the furnace, looking towards the creek to the south, the level terrace extended for a further 11 metres, where the fan-shaped casting-floor was marked out by stones set on edge on the east and west sides.

The cold blast was supplied by an imported American blower powered by a 10-horsepower steam-engine.[9] The evidence on the site for the placing of the blower is not as clear as for all other features of the operation, but it is likely that, as at Lal Lal, it was on the level above the foundations of the blast-furnace. Many features of Bogolong closely resemble the Lal Lal plant of 1881 and this would certainly be the most convenient arrangement. As at Lal Lal, the blower could not be placed under the loading bridge. It was probably sited to the west where a large gum tree (the only one close to the furnace) could have drawn its initial nutrients from the ash deposit of the burnt fuel, just as at Joadja (a major oil-shale site) every stone fireplace in a row of 19 vanished cottages has nurtured a pseudo-acacia.

The furnace itself was a tapering stone tower projecting 4 metres above a base 3.4 metres square and 2.1 metres high, made of stone rubble, including some handsome bluestone. Two masons, James White and James Burns, lived

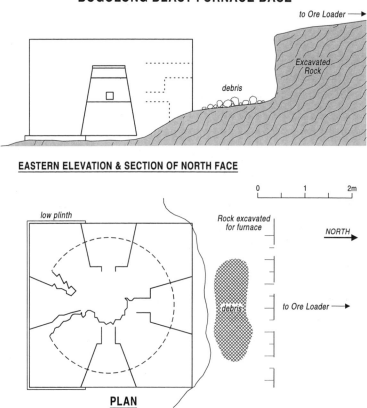

BOGOLONG BLAST FURNACE BASE

EASTERN ELEVATION & SECTION OF NORTH FACE

PLAN

Plan of the blast-furnace base and elevation with the northern tuyere recess shown in dotted outline. (A. Cremin and University of Sydney Cartography)

in the Bookham area in the 1870s:[10] if this is their work, it is undistinguished but sturdy and is still standing when so many other structures have vanished.

The placing of the furnace is very close indeed to the cardinal points of the compass. In each face of the base there is a well-constructed recess, not arched as at Lal Lal or Ilfracombe, but squared off with a wooden lintel. These lintels still have bark upon their upper surfaces and may have been off-cuts from the large logs cut square to provide the main timbers of the loading bridge. The cold blast was supplied through three tuyeres within the east, north and west recesses. Probably each connecting pipe sloped upwards externally from the tuyere opening, in a gooseneck lying along the angled stone within the upper part of the recess, to link with the main blast-pipe coming down (as at Lal Lal) under the last stage of the trestle-bridge. The tuyere holes and their surrounds are made of brick.

The bricks were the joker in the Bogolong pack. The syndicate's builders chose to use local fire-bricks made on a property in the adjacent parish of Woolgarlo. This squatting property, owned by the Robinsons, was a cattle-run,[11] occupied in 1875 only by the squatter, his stockman and, unexpectedly, a miner called James Porter. There was a brick-maker in Binalong to the north,[12] but the exploitation of a fire-clay pit on Woolgarlo station is undocumented

Bogolong blast-furnace from the north-east, showing the tuyere recess in the east face of the base. Near the top of the 6-metre-high tower is one of the beam-holes for the loading bridge. (R. Ian Jack, 1993)

Bogolong blast-furnace: interior of the east tuyere, showing the wooden lintel and the fire-brick tuyere hole in the centre back. (R. Ian Jack, 1993)

save for Bogolong's disastrous decision reported in the Albury press.[13] What happened at the first smelting on 31 March 1874 was graphically told. 'Unfortunately, the firebricks from Woolgarlo burst away over the tuyrers [sic], and ran together at the tymp-hole, causing a cessation of the work.' As a result the syndicate intended 'to obtain sound firebricks at once from Sydney, with a view to thoroughly testing the venture'.[14] Despite the accident, five pigs were cast on 31 March and sent to Albury and on to Melbourne.[15]

Some repairs must have been made quickly, for there was a second smelt seven weeks later, on 20 May 1874, when four pigs were cast in moulds bearing the Bogolong name and sent, like those of 31 March, to Melbourne via Albury.[16] The evidence of the furnace today suggests that there was little, if any, replacement of the original bricks with Sydney fire-bricks. The coating of the crucible, above the hearth, has been partly removed through the broken south tap hole entry and shows poor-quality bricks partly exploded, coated on both sides with a thin deposit of iron and slag. The iron being smelted had clearly broken into part of the clay packing between the fire-brick lining and the stone cladding, and the remains seem more compatible with the accident at the first smelting than with the second. We conclude therefore that the repairs to the furnace were inadequate and that the closure of the furnace after the second smelt was caused by continuing structural difficulties rather than the need to form 'a company with sufficient capital, and on a scale adequate to the working of the mine', prepared to erect 'a more extensive plant'.[17] The projected Bogolong Charcoal Ironworks Company failed to materialize, the original furnace was simply abandoned, and, since it is doing no harm to person or to stock, it has survived through the subdivision of the iron lease area to the Garry family in the 1880s to the further redistribution in the late 1900s among the Arabins. The fire-bricks have been robbed from inside the furnace, almost to the top, leaving their impression in the clay packing—so someone must have felt that Woolgarlo brick had some potential. All the moveable equipment has gone: we found only one small galvanized-iron sheet which may have been part of the structures around the engine or the casting-bed.

The men who established this impressive ruin have left no traces of habitation, although some names may be suggested for them. In the 1872 directory for the area there were no fewer than six miners among a total of 90 listed residents. John Williams lived on Bogolong station, James Porter on Woolgarlo and James O'Brien on Stony Creek. The other three—James Miles, William Tully and Henry Ewington—had no specific location. Four of these were still in the area in 1875, after the ironworks closed; John Williams and Henry Ewington were no longer included.[18] These miners may have been primarily gold-seekers on the Cumbamurra River gold-field immediately to the north-west,[19] but they constituted the local labour pool which the Bogolong syndicate would have wished to tap.

The syndicate did not persevere. Albury, unlike Melbourne and Ballarat, which financed Tamar and Lal Lal, had no large-scale foundries or manufacturing industry and did not itself provide a market for locally produced iron.[20] The Melbourne investors who might have subscribed to the Bogolong company were simultaneously involved in expensive and unproductive investments in Tasmania while in Sydney what interest in iron there was concentrated on the attempted resurgence of Fitzroy in 1874–5 or Rutherford's new Eskbank in 1875–6.

So Bogolong furnace was left alone. The traditional belief in Binalong today is that it was used for melting down bushrangers' gold. In the country still proud of John Gilbert and Ben Hall, this is understandable and every monument should acquire a folklore. But both Gilbert and Hall were shot dead in the mid-1860s and never saw the blast-furnace. Bogolong furnace produced nine pigs of iron and not a single ingot of gold.

CHAPTER SIX

CREATING A STEEL TOWN:
LITHGOW,
NEW SOUTH WALES

Ever since the fastnesses of the Blue Mountains were violated by successive lines of road—William Cox's in 1814, Lawson's Long Alley and Archibald Bell's in 1823, Edmund Lockyer's in 1829, Thomas Mitchell's Victoria Pass in 1832—the area now occupied by the City of Greater Lithgow has been both a place of settlement and a staging post to the western plains. Though beyond the mountains, Lithgow lies quite high (1000 metres above sea-level) and its land is pastoral rather than agricultural. Crops have been grown from the earliest time of settlement in the 1820s, but cattle and sheep have always been dominant.

The geography of settlement was largely conditioned by the success of Victoria Pass, which in the 1830s brought westward traffic for the first time through Hartley instead of Hartley Vale. Collitt's Inn at Hartley Vale, built in 1823, was superseded by a veritable row of inns built during the two decades following 1832 in or around the new village of Bowenfels on the Great Western Highway. Although the village proper did have a small grid pattern, lying between the Presbyterian Church to the north and the National School to the south on the western side of the highway, the settlement was essentially a ribbon of houses, farms and inns straggling along the highway from Fernhill to Cooerwull.

This general character of Bowenfels is unchanged, and a great wealth of architectural heritage survives, but its context was disrupted by the sudden and frenetic growth of an Industrial-Revolution town in the adjacent valley. Although Hassans Walls present a dramatic buffer between South Bowenfels and Lithgow, the north end of Bowenfels, where Cooerwull estate dominated colonial development, abuts upon the industrial valley and accordingly that northern portion of the village has seen far greater change than the southern part.

Today, as one drives north along the highway from Bowenfels Presbyterian Church, past Lithgow General Cemetery, there is a sharp transition into much newer housing. Further north again, Main Street enters the highway from the east; to turn down Main Street into Lithgow Valley is to enter a very different streetscape and the ambience of an industrial town.

Lithgow was created because of its coal deposits. Several seams of coal outcrop in the steep walls of the valleys in the area, and this was, of course, well known to the early settlers. Andrew Brown of Cooerwull mined coal on his own estate, primarily to feed the boiler of his flour and tweed mill, from the 1850s onwards; while Thomas Brown of Eskbank, actually in Lithgow Valley, also exploited his coal seam in the 1860s for domestic needs. The fireplaces of Bowenfels used coal as well as wood. The development, however, from a purely local supplier of fuel to a major commercial industry with high capitalization could come only with the railway.

The opening of the Zig-Zag, one of the great feats of railway engineering in the colonial world, transformed Lithgow Valley.[1] After 1869 it was no longer a sparsely occupied area adjacent to Bowenfels. Instead it became, within four or five years from 1869, a boom town, completely overshadowing Bowenfels. The rail link to the coast meant that coal could be sent to the city and overseas, but more importantly the railway to Sydney and the west offered the prospect of lucrative, permanent contracts for engine-fuel.

The railway had one further direct effect. Iron rails were needed in great quantity, first for laying the track and thereafter for maintaining it and building industrial sidings. So the concept of establishing a major foundry and, as an extension of that idea, a blast-furnace to smelt iron ore using the abundant Lithgow coal, seemed singularly attractive. Thus, while Lithgow Valley, the Hermitage, the Vale of Clwydd and Eskbank collieries all increased production in the 1870s, James Rutherford, of Cobb and Co. fame, thought it worthwhile in 1874 to build a blast-furnace on Thomas Brown's land. Although this enterprise for smelting iron failed, the foundry continued, using mainly railway scrap-iron to make recycled rails. The first steel in Australia was produced at Eskbank in 1900 and the ironmaster, William Sandford, invested in a new blast-furnace in 1906–7, immediately having to sell to the Hoskins brothers when the bank foreclosed on his substantial mortgage.

The superficial attractiveness of coal supplies on the spot—the entrance of Eskbank coal-mine was only yards from Sandford's foundry—lured other industries to the town. Copper was refined in Lithgow by no fewer than three separate companies; the Lloyd company brought partly processed copper regulus from its mine out in the bush at Burraga, while the Great Cobar Company brought its blister copper all the way from Cobar. Although both Lloyd and Great Cobar were vigorous in the first decade of this century, only Lloyd (transmuted into Mouramba) survived the First World War.

The famous pottery attached to Lithgow Valley Colliery suffered a similar fate, with great achievements in the period of 1879 to 1896 and a brief, final revival under Arthur Brownfield from 1905 to 1907. Like some of the brick-works, which were created to meet the building needs of the community, the more mundane activities of the pipe-making aspect of the Lithgow Valley Pottery lasted longer: the pipeworks was dismantled only in 1946 and the last of the Lithgow brickworks, the Scenic, formerly the Vale of Clwydd, was closed by the State Pollution Control Commission only in 1977.[2]

Optimistic belief in the virtue of raw materials transformed the valley into an industrial scene, bustling with supporting services, new housing, shops and businesses in the last three decades of the nineteenth century. One new venture combined the old pastoralism with the new industrialization: in 1873 the great and ingenious Thomas Sutcliffe Mort built a meat-processing factory, using his newfangled refrigeration plant to dispatch the carcasses by rail. Two breweries opened, banks blossomed: the *Lithgow Mercury* soon had a business directory on its front page. New coal-mines opened: the Zig-Zag in 1883, Oakey Park and New Vale in 1889, Great Cobar in 1899.

The population of Lithgow increased steadily: in 1881 it was 2112; in 1891, 3865; in 1901, 5268; in 1911, after the opening of Sandford's blast-furnace, 8196.

THE DEVELOPMENT OF LITHGOW, 1869–84

Lithgow was created because it had coal in abundance and, after 1869, a rail-way to the coast running right down the valley. Since several seams of coal outcrop in the steep walls of Lithgow Valley, the early pastoralists in the area were aware of the possibilities. Andrew Brown of Cooerwull to the west had mined coal on his estate from the 1850s onwards; Thomas Brown of Eskbank was exploiting his coal measures by the 1860s.[3] The critical development of transforming this domestic supply into a major industry with considerable capitalization was the opening of the Zig-Zag railway in 1869. The rail link allowed the movement of heavy goods such as coal to the markets of the coast. Also, as the railway continued to extend inland to Bathurst and to Mudgee, Lithgow was in a critically important position to provide coal to refuel the steam trains on their extended schedules, with no freight charges at all incurred by mine owners.[4]

Since iron rails were required for laying the main-line track, for establishing industrial sidings within Lithgow and for replacing worn-out rails as the traffic on the western line increased in volume, a major foundry to manufacture these rails in Lithgow was an attractive proposition. The leading entrepreneurs who created the Eskbank Iron Works Co. in 1874 were James Rutherford, the American owner of Cobb & Co., and Dan Williams, a railway contractor, in conjunction with John Sutherland, a leading cabinet min-

Aerial photograph of Lithgow, showing how the railway bisects the valley. The blast-furnace site is the diamond-shaped site towards the top right-hand corner, at the foot of a very wooded hill.

ister under Sir Henry Parkes and Sir John Robertson. Rutherford, with Sutherland as managing director, built rolling-mills for the manufacture of rails from scrap-iron, but decided also to attempt to exploit the iron ore contained in clay-bands among the Lithgow Valley seams and to smelt his own pig-iron for his own foundry.[5]

The site chosen by Rutherford for the integrated operation of smelting and rolling was on Thomas Brown's Eskbank estate, close to the coal-mine opened by Brown. This ironworks was bounded by Farmer's Creek to the north, and by the streets now known as Tank Street, to the east, Read Avenue and Hoskins Avenue to the south. On this large level site in 1875–6 Rutherford erected a blast-furnace to smelt local ores, but, because of initial competition from a revived Fitzroy smelter and the low price of imported iron, the Lithgow blast-furnace failed to prosper. After a tentative beginning

Rutherford's Eskbank blast-furnace. (State Library of Victoria H 15317)

in 1878–9 its production of pig-iron had increased sharply in 1880–2 once a contract for government rails had been signed and once the 'first roller ever cast in Australia for the purpose of rolling full-weight railway iron'[6] had been installed.

Pig-iron production (in tons)

1878	389
1879	118
1880	1200
1881	2737
1882	4320

The raw materials were largely local: iron from the clay-bands in the valley (supplemented by ore from Clarence, above the Zig-Zag, from Mount Wilson and from Blayney which was reached by the railway in 1876), limestone from the valley but more particularly from Piper's Flat, 22 kilometres away on the railway line, and coal literally on site, converted into usable coke in Rutherford's own coke ovens.[7]

The problems which Rutherford faced were greater than these advantages: the iron ore was of uncertain quality and the freight charges to Sydney for his pig-iron or rolled sheets were high enough to make his product uncompetitive. Accordingly Rutherford decided to make an end of his blast-furnace in 1884. 'Not to be tempted in the future',[8] as he said, he not only closed the blast-furnace in July 1884 but brought two carts of gunpowder and blew it up.[9] This was the end of large-scale iron-smelting in New South Wales for nearly a quarter of a century, but it was not the end of iron-making at Lithgow under Rutherford and the site remained in use as a foundry and rolling-mill until 1932. The development of this ironworks, moreover, is a vital part of the history of the later blast-furnace on another site. The continuity between Rutherford's blast-furnace-cum-ironworks and the blast-furnace of 1906–28, a kilometre to the south-east, is quite simply one man, William Sandford.

WILLIAM SANDFORD

William Sandford was a complex and troubled man. He was not a 'restless Titan' as Geoffrey Blainey described Essington Lewis of BHP,[10] but he was a man whose struggle with self-doubt and with unyielding economic facts had about it something of the heroic.

Like Essington Lewis, Sandford had a background more rural than industrial, and he never forgot his horticultural youth, finally coming full cycle when his days as an ironmaster came so abruptly to an end. The Sandfords had been in Torrington in North Devon for generations, running market gardens 'producing flowers, fruits and vegetables';[11] both William Sandford's father and brother were gardeners and seedsmen in Torrington[12] and William in his formative years in the 1840s and 1850s must have been very familiar indeed with the business of horticulture. William moved away from Devon, gained business experience as an accountant and as a bank-clerk, before entering the iron-foundry business as secretary to the Ashton Gate Ironworks in Bristol.[13] His brother Robert, who remained in Torrington, showed entrepreneurial flair, and in 1874, while retaining his gardening interests, established a major butter factory in Torrington. By the time William moved to Australia in 1883 Robert and his son had enlarged the Torridge Vale Butter Factory to supply Devon dairy and poultry products the length and breadth of England.[14] There were many parallels between Robert and William Sandford, for their respective capacities did not regularly match their charismatic vision.

William came to Australia in 1883 to manage a wire-netting plant for John Lysaght, the English maker of Orb galvanized-iron who had opened his first Australian agency three years previously, in Melbourne.[15] Sandford's zeal for the iron industry in Australia was not, perhaps, the primary reason for his emigration. His marriage had failed in England and he abandoned his wife and two children to come to Sydney; within months of his arrival he was married to another woman, Caroline Newey, herself previously married.[16] There are a number of unanswered questions about these adventures: certainly the first Mrs Sandford was still alive in England 20 years later and, although William kept in touch with his English son Jack, who worked as his overseas agent, he confessed in a letter to his son-in-law, 'I cannot expect Jack or his sister to have any good feelings towards me'.[17]

He referred in the same letter of 1904 to the second Mrs Sandford as 'my children's mother here . . . very much put out over the position of her children' and in his Australian will he blandly ignored the existence of any children other than the two sons and a daughter by his Australian wife.[18] His second marriage was by no means an unqualified success, but William and Caroline remained partners for 48 years despite a series of separations around the halfway mark. It seems likely that Sandford was pulled to Australia by an emotional crisis in 1883 as much as by a missionary zeal to improve iron production.

None the less, he quickly developed an enthusiasm for ironworks in Australia and after three years he left Lysaght and took over the lease of the Fitzroy ironworks at Mittagong in 1886. At that time no Australian iron ore was being smelted into pig-iron anywhere in Australia—Fitzroy had not smelted since 1877, while Lal Lal in Victoria and Rutherford's blast-furnace at Lithgow had both ceased in 1884—so Sandford's interest first in Mittagong and then in Lithgow was initially only in rolling-mills, which continued to function using scrap-iron instead of locally made pig-iron. Such experience as he had had in England and with Lysaght's products in Australia, was, after all, with rolling-mills, and as a manager rather than as a technical expert.

In 1886 the Fitzroy ironworks at Mittagong and Rutherford's surviving mills at Lithgow had equal shares in the all-important government contract for rolling rails and Sandford saw that neither could afford to compete in this way. So he transferred the Fitzroy share to Lithgow and himself became general manager at Lithgow in 1886. In this slightly crab-wise fashion William Sandford came to Lithgow and began his critically important 20-year domination of the Lithgow scene and the New South Wales iron industry.[19]

In 1887, confirmed in 1890, he leased the works from Rutherford for an initial seven-year period, earning a nominal salary of £5 a week and a set share of the profits.[20] The following year he sued Rutherford over cash amounting to £7500 paid by the railway commissioners as part of a deal cancelling the rail contract. Rutherford simply pocketed this cash settlement but after Sandford had commenced his equity suit agreed to pay Sandford £3250 and to allow him to profit from the sale of 10000 tonnes of old rails.[21]

In 1892, soon after this financial skirmish, Sandford bought the entire Eskbank works outright from Rutherford and his partners. By this time the Eskbank Company owned not only the ironworks and inactive ore leases in various locations but also Eskbank Colliery and the late Thomas Brown's Eskbank estate. This consolidation of property was of prime importance for the future, since the undeveloped land in the valley where Brown's stock had grazed could gradually be subdivided and sold off to create a workmen's community.[22]

Sandford's grand purchase of 1892 was characteristic of the man. All the elements which can be observed in the period 1905 to 1907 are there: large vision, invincible optimism and under-capitalization. As Rutherford recalled at the end of his life in 1911, Sandford in 1892

> had no money and the Commercial Bank offered to advance him £5000 …
> [The executors of Rutherford's former partner, Dan Williams] would not accept
> a deposit of less than £12000. I could not put up with the men and other work
> demanded my attention, so, to make up the sale, I went to the Bank and made
> myself personally responsible for £7000 to make up the £12000. Then, of
> course, I ran it the same as before, I paid all the wages, and everything went
> through me. The total amount of the purchase money was £7000—although
> the property was worth £150000—and in three years Mr Sandford got around
> the Bank and had the £7000 reduced to £3000, and the Bank advanced him
> the money then, and paid him off. That was the end of my association with the
> iron-works.[23]

Sandford had become an independent ironmaster during the depression of the 1890s, but the growing productivity of the metal industry catering for the late Victorian expansion of population, agrarian exploitation, mining of all sorts and railway engineering protected Sandford from the worst effects of the general slump. As a result he was able to expand the rolling-mills at Eskbank in a variety of typically *ad hoc* ways.

At the same time, he dreamt of establishing a blast-furnace to smelt the ores over which he held leases. He realized that iron-smelting would remain unprofitable unless there was a tariff on imported pig-iron to protect the local product. In his private notebook, as early as January 1893, just after he had begun the purchase of Eskbank, he was mulling over the revival of iron-smelting there: 'If a Protective tariff is introduced an Agency must be had in Sydney—Try small Blast Furnace and Steel plant make 100 tons Rails week-ly 5000 tons annually.'[24]

Up to this time steel had not been made in Australia. Steel could perfectly well be processed from imported or reused iron; the making of steel did not have as a necessary corollary the re-establishment of a colonial smelting oper-ation. The capital outlay to import a small steel-making furnace was, more-over, much lower than the establishment of a blast-furnace to smelt iron ore. In 1898, therefore, Sandford decided to go ahead with importing a steel plant.[25]

Already some deterioration in his self-confidence and possibly even men-tal health was becoming evident in Sandford's private diaries. In the previous year, 1897, he had gone to see William Warren, the foundation professor of

William Sandford in 1908. Detail of the portrait by Norman Carter now in the BHP collection. (R. Ian Jack)

Engineering at the University of Sydney, and had admonished himself in his diary: 'Want self-confidence. Self sufficient. Be a gentleman … Calm Quiet thoughtful Civil Firm.'[26] In March 1898 Sandford was writing privately: 'Caution in speaking my thoughts. Any expression when once spoken to another becomes my master. Before it is spoken I am its Master—Caution caution.'[27]

He had real enough worries with his overdraft and the expense of running Eskroy, an 11-room country house with 526 hectares of land,[28] but quelled his uncertainties sufficiently in 1900 to buy a 4-tonne Siemens-Martin open-hearth furnace to manufacture steel at Eskbank.[29]

The output was small but the symbolic significance for the new century and for federated Australia was enormous. Sandford, who had a good eye for publicity and always used the public spectacle skilfully, made the most of becoming a steelmaster as well as an ironmaster. He organized a grand banquet and invited many prominent people from Sydney to witness the first tapping of steel in Australia on 25 April 1900.[30]

Sandford was no longer young: he celebrated his sixtieth birthday in 1901, 17 months after the successful operation of the steel furnace. The steps which he took to re-establish the processing of Australian iron ore were increasingly hesitant, though never unthoughtful. Sandford had been aware of the potential of building a blast-furnace for many years: he had succeeded to Mittagong when its blast-furnace was still in existence and knew how Rutherford had demolished the Lithgow blast-furnace two years earlier. In

The Eskbank Iron and Steelworks in 1905, from a publicity brochure. (Mitchell Library (ML), Small Picture File)

January 1893 he had percipiently noted in his private diary that a protective tariff would encourage iron-smelting.[31] He had contemplated a government plant in Lithgow in 1897[32] and had been reinforced in his vision by Charles Hoskins, with whom he shared a sea-passage from Western Australia in 1899.[33] In 1902 he brought out to Australia a Welsh consulting engineer called Enoch James, who reported optimistically on the quality of local ores, gave a plan for a blast-furnace complex and an unrealistically low estimate of the costs.[34]

The following years were full of worry and, in his diaries, self-exhortations: 'I must be calm, thoughtful and earnest. Not given to wine or spirituous liquors'[35]—this two years after he had told his son: 'In order to have a clear head, I have almost given up taking any stimulants.'[36] In 1903 Sandford complained that 'my bodily health is good, but my Head is bad again',[37] and in 1906 he confided to his diary: 'I forget things so quickly—awful job I cannot depend on myself.'[38]

As he vacillated over the building of the blast-furnace, his financial worries, real or imaginary—but mostly real—increased. He thought of returning to the horticulture of his youth. He had already in the 1890s stocked Eskroy with a large number of fruit trees—plum, apple and pear—as well as raspberries and gooseberries,[39] and in 1905 was disposed to 'irrigate and manure—quietly and thoughtfully go on my way'.[40] Simultaneously he was called upon to assist his brother Robert and the widow of another brother, both still in Torrington. Robert had diversified into acquiring the major flour mills in Torrington near his butter factory and had lost £1200 in the venture. William had invested in

Robert's enterprise and had shared in his difficulties. He assisted his sister-in-law, remained on friendly terms with Robert and sent his sister £10 at Christmas. 'Torrington,' he remarked sadly to his son Jack, 'is a poor place now [1906]. At the same time, I don't see that I should carry their burdens. Their wants are few.'[41]

Robert Sandford too was failing. 'Owing to increasing age [he] had not the energy to enlarge the business or provide further development' and the Torridge Vale factory was ultimately sold to Cow & Gate, who transformed the plant in the 1930s.[42] William Sandford did find the energy for the great development of Lithgow in 1906–7 but failed more dramatically than his brother.

In mid-1903 James had supplied Sandford with detailed drawings of a proposed plant, with four blast-furnaces, each with four stoves and, initially, four boilers. He also gave a suggested location for coke ovens and for a steelworks adjacent to the blast-furnace. The plans were drawn up for a site very close to Eskbank House, to the west of Inch Street, a site which Sandford rejected in favour of the present site to the east of Inch Street. Sandford and his next consultant, the Middlesbrough engineer Joseph Harrison, also rejected some of James' layout and greatly reduced the initial expenditure; but the concept put forward by James is clearly evident in Sandford's own sketch-plan of March 1906.[43] After returning to Wales via China, where James also reported for the Chinese government on its deposits of iron ore, he wrote to Sandford at the end of 1904, saying: 'I am as fully persuaded now as ever that your scheme has the elements of great success and the natural conditions with regard to material are unsurpassed anywhere.'[44]

James had not only encouraged Sandford in 1902 to proceed to build a new blast-furnace but also costed the pig-iron produced at only 35 shillings a ton. This price was entirely unrealistic, given the high cost of Australian labour and the fact that imported pig-iron was selling for more than 35 shillings in 1903.[45] But Sandford believed James' estimate and accordingly set about buying a blast-furnace, anticipating either a tariff on imports or a bounty on his product to make profit-making possible. Although Jack, Sandford's son by his first marriage, was looking after Eskbank interests in Britain, William Sandford took himself off to England (in what was clearly a series of overseas business tours) in 1902 and placed an order for a blast-furnace while there.[46] No doubt because of the failure of the new federal parliament to accept the proposed Iron Bonus Bill and the inactivation of the 1902 Tariff Act, which merely enabled a governor-general to impose tariffs on imported iron, Sandford did not seek to have his blast-furnace shipped to Australia and indeed went so far in 1904 as to ask Jack Sandford to sell it off in England (an order which was quickly countermanded).[47]

The critical turning point came when the state government of New South

Wales, under Carruthers, agreed to tender for a contract designed unashamedly to suit Sandford and no one else. The terms of the proposed contract in June 1905 were:

> The contractor shall establish, within the State of New South Wales, blast furnace, or blast furnaces, and erect all machinery and plant necessary for the conversion of iron ore into pig iron and rolled steel and iron, capable of supplying all the materials included in the contract. The whole of the pig iron supplied to the Government of New South Wales and 90% of the pig iron used in the manufacture of materials to be supplied under the contract is to be produced from ore raised in the Commonwealth of Australia.[48]

Sandford was the sole tenderer and a seven-year contract was signed on 21 October 1905. The price agreed upon after negotiation for locally smelted pig-iron was unrealistically low at £3.15.0 a ton, but since this was £2 a ton higher than Enoch James' 1902 estimate it seemed acceptable to Sandford. So although he was assured of a steady market for his product, he was not in fact assured of the necessary profit to cover the high cost of capitalization and labour.[49]

Sandford acted vigorously and decisively. The seven-year contract was to come into operation on 1 June 1907, so there was need for rapid action. Only two days after the signing of the contract in October 1905, Sandford's ironworks manager, William Thornley, sailed for America and England on his third overseas trip. As Sandford noted in his private diary four weeks before Thornley left: 'During the last 7 years I have been five times around the world, have seen the very latest improvement in Iron & Steel producing. Manager has been twice so that we are alive to all that is going on.'[50]

Thornley advised the purchase of a furnace in England (presumably not the furnace purchased in 1904) under the planning oversight of Joseph Harrison, the consulting engineer in the great iron town of Middlesbrough.[51] Thornley also engaged an experienced blast-furnace manager from Blaenavon in Monmouthshire, Percy Pennymore, who arrived in Lithgow in April 1906.[52]

Much of Sandford's concept was firmly based on his own exposure in 1902 to the great Belgian complex at Seraing.[53] The Cockerill brothers from Britain had opened the first plant at Seraing in 1814 and built the first coke-fired blast-furnaces in Belgium ten years later. The Cockerill enterprise in the old bishop's palace of Seraing was still a showpiece of European industry in the early twentieth century; for Sandford it was a model of integration, with the iron-producing plant adjacent to the steel-producing furnaces, to the roller-mills and to the coke ovens.[54] Sandford was perfectly well aware of the advantages of such a plan.

CHAPTER SEVEN

THE LITHGOW

BLAST-FURNACES

Sandford's decision to locate the new blast-furnace on a site one kilometre away from the existing ironworks/steelworks has been much criticized, since iron smelted at the blast-furnace had to be transported to the steel furnaces far away. There are, however, two factors which mitigate this criticism. One is that Sandford always expected to manufacture pig-iron and to sell his product in that form to coastal customers such as the Hoskins brothers. From that point of view a site adjacent to the main railway line from Sydney was an advantage. The government's coal stage on the main line immediately adjacent to the new blast-furnace had been in operation since 1888 and had its own siding, a dump road, conveniently sited on the north side of the main line. It was therefore particularly convenient and cheap for Sandford to extend this dump road in September 1906 with his own private sidings for the delivery of raw materials and the dispatch of the anticipated pig-iron from the new works. It is true that the ironworks had been linked to the main line by a much longer series of sidings since 1878, but there is no doubt that the choice of the coal stage for the blast-furnace was in itself a good one.[1]

The second mitigating factor in judging Sandford's wisdom in his choice of site grows out of the first; further, it is even more important and seems to be entirely unknown to earlier researchers of Sandford and Hoskins. Sandford's initial plans involved not only a blast-furnace on this new, convenient site but also the erection of new steel furnaces. The mountain was to be brought to Mahomet. On 10 March 1906, only 12 days before work began on the new site, Sandford drew an annotated plan of his intended plant, showing not only all the features which were in fact erected—blast-furnace, heating stoves and boilers—but also the position of steel furnaces and steel rolling-mills to the east of the blast-furnace.[2] Ten days later, when the local surveyor, Mylecharane, was pegging out the site, Sandford was

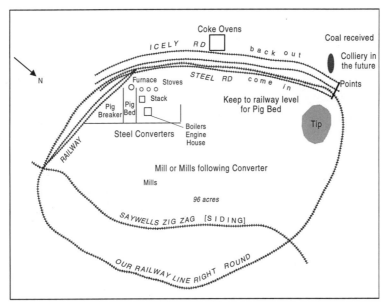

Adaptation of Sandford's sketch of an integrated ironworks, with blast-furnaces, coke ovens and steel mills. (University of Sydney cartography based on ML Sandford papers MSS1556/1/4)

firmly intending to install a Siemens open-hearth furnace for making steel, along with cogging, roughing and finishing steel mills, with the further addition of wire-rod mills and plant for wire and netting (which would have brought him back full cycle to his work with Lysaght in 1883–5).[3]

As late as 28 December 1906, when the blast-furnace was well advanced, Sandford was still working at very practical plans for building a battery of a dozen or more steel furnaces immediately below the tap hole level of the blast-furnace, so that the ladle containing the freshly smelted molten iron could deftly top-load the new furnaces.[4]

There is no doubt, therefore, that Sandford was well aware of the economic desirability of integrating processing plant and iron-smelting on the one site, which had been done at Lithgow in Rutherford's time and was later done at Newcastle by BHP and at Port Kembla by Hoskins, but which was never achieved at Lithgow by either Sandford or Hoskins. The further capital expense involved in installing steel furnaces was beyond Sandford's resources, as the cost of the blast-furnace proper spiralled upwards from his optimistic £30 000 to £100 000.

The levelling of Coal Stage Hill began on 22 March 1906 with picks and shovels, later supplemented by half a tonne of gelignite. The excavation, as it was noted on 3 April, 'will make provision only for the first blast furnace and necessary engine, boilers and stoves'. The additional steel furnaces and the possible additional blast-furnaces (Sandford, like James, thought of up to four in all) would call for excavation at some later date.[5]

Construction work on the site on 8 June 1906. The stove bases are well advanced, with vertical formwork visible at centre. Immediately in front of them is the foundation of the furnace on which several men are standing. At the back the rail line at left and Inch Street at right converge and run together towards the town visible at the extreme right, overshadowed by steam from one of the copper smelters. (ML, PXA149)

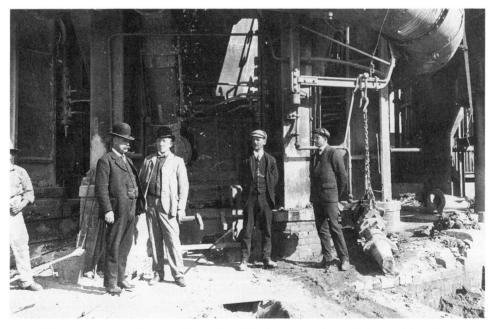

The managers standing on either side of the iron tap hole at the base of the blast-furnace; the tap hole gun is visible on the ground at the right. From left, W. Thornley, W. Sandford, P. Pennymore and Sandford's son Roy. May 1907. (ML, Small Picture File)

It was a time of feverish activity for the managerial staff, Thornley and Pennymore. The first two boilers arrived in Sydney from Babcock & Wilcox in Britain in April;[6] the ironworks was busy casting the ten I-columns, each weighing almost seven tonnes, to support the blast-furnace;[7] in June thousands of bricks were delivered for the foundations of the furnaces and stoves, for the high engine-house and for the main chimney stack;[8] the new railway sidings were installed in September.[9] It was all strikingly efficient.

The late decision to install a supplementary blowing-engine as an insurance against the failure of the 120-tonne Davy engine imported from Sheffield resulted from Sandford's visit to Mount Morgan in Queensland in July 1906. Like Mount Morgan Mines, Sandford ordered a Parsons turbo-blower from England, and by the end of November 1906 excavations were under way for the foundations of a second engine-house immediately to the south of the Davy house.[10]

For his supply of fuel, Sandford entered into an agreement with Oakey Park colliery nearby, which had more than doubled its coke-oven capacity in anticipation of a standing order from the blast-furnace.[11] But Sandford had a firm commitment to building his own coke ovens when his financial position was stabilized. On the plan of the site which he drew in March 1906, he showed a site for future coke ovens on the west side of Inch Street:[12] as early as 1901 Sandford had received a plan for advanced coke ovens from Brussels[13] and in 1902 he had been impressed by the ovens at Seraing, also in Belgium.[14]

For the moment, however, Sandford was content to buy local coke, and coke ovens were not constructed on the site (at the east end) until 1911–12, by Charles Hoskins. Limestone presented no problem, with good deposits at Portland along the western railway.

Iron ore could no longer, as in Rutherford's time, be extracted in suitable quantity or quality from the Lithgow area, and the deposits at Carcoar, on Coombing Park estate, were already on lease to Sandford. The Carcoar lease had originally been held by Rutherford and his partners, one of whom, W. F. Whitney, was the owner of Coombing Park, and this lease was included in the sale of Eskbank to Sandford by Rutherford in 1892. Sandford had some justifiable doubts about the quality of the Carcoar ore, but went ahead with the construction of a rail link between Carcoar and the main line, employed 60 men in the re-opened mine and during 1907 railed 34 500 tonnes of ore to Lithgow.[15]

There is no doubt that the official opening of the blast-furnace by the Premier of New South Wales on 13 May 1907 was the proudest moment of Sandford's life, crowning the years of achievement begun with the making of steel seven years before. Prudently, the blast-furnace had been lit well ahead of the official opening: Mrs Pennymore had kindled it on 28 April, Sandford's daughter Clarice started the blast on 30 April and the first tapping

Formal opening of the blast-furnace, 13 May 1907. (ML, PXA149)

of pig-iron was done later the same day. The plant which was feted on 13 May by guests arriving on special trains from Sydney was therefore already proven to be in working order and the small tapping done that day was not attended by the embarrassing delays experienced at the opening of the first steel furnace.[16]

The triumph was peculiarly Sandford's own, for he had constructed the blast-furnace as a private individual. The company, William Sandford Ltd, which owned the ironworks/steelworks, did not own the blast-furnace. The overdraft of £63 500 incurred in the new works was therefore a private liability of Sandford himself. The company, however, had the government contract, and to fulfil this it decided to purchase the blast-furnace plant from Sandford as well as those parts of the Eskbank estate, including the colliery, which were still privately owned by Sandford. On 8 May 1907, between the lighting of the blast-furnace and its official opening, the company purchased both the blast-furnace site and the Eskbank estate for a total of £75 683, paid to Sandford in company shares, under an agreement dated 28 June 1907.[17]

The company, William Sandford Ltd, was seriously under-capitalized and, despite an overdraft with the Commercial Bank of £131 078, was still short of liquid capital to the tune of at least £50 000. The federal government still failed to provide a bonus to iron-makers, and by October Sandford realized that he could not fulfil the government order for pig-iron without additional capital and sought a state government loan of £70 000.[18] Financial advisers counselled the government against this on business grounds and there was criticism of the quality of management at the blast-furnace, but political considerations were also important and the state cabinet on 22 November agreed, subject to the consent of parliament, to make the advance of £70 000 to William Sandford Ltd with generous repayment conditions spread over ten years. This offer followed negotiations with the Commercial

Bank over the problem of Sandford's mortgage, and a compromise had been hammered out that the government's mortgage would take precedence over the bank's only to the extent of £25 000 should foreclosure on the company assets become necessary.[19]

On 4 December 1907 the Legislative Assembly debated the loan and approved it, but with one critical amendment. The Labor opposition successfully amended the details so that the whole government loan of £70 000 had priority over the bank's loan of £131 000 in the event of foreclosure. In these circumstances, the Commercial Bank, in its own protection, foreclosed on William Sandford Ltd.[20] This resulted in the closure of the ironworks/steelworks on 8 December but, to preserve the bank's investment, the blast-furnace continued to operate, as internal damage might be caused by sudden blowing out.[21] There was consternation in Lithgow; the association of the smelter-workers at the blast-furnace tried to organize the combined Lithgow iron unions, accustomed to co-operative enterprise at Eskbank, into paying £50 000 as part of a rescue bid.[22]

On 11 December Charles Hoskins entered the scene, by a back door. He and his brother George had, since 1875, run a major iron foundry in Sydney and had established the firm, Hoskins Bros, as the chief manufacturer of iron pipes in Australia. It was Charles Hoskins with whom Sandford had discussed the future of iron-making as they sailed from Fremantle to Sydney in 1899;[23] it was Hoskins to whom Sandford had talked in May 1906, when Charles advised him to be his 'own boss, have no partners';[24] Hoskins Bros was one of the largest real and anticipated customers of Lithgow-made pig-iron; and Charles was already a shareholder, with 1000 shares in William Sandford Ltd.[25]

Charles Hoskins. (Hoskins' 'Black Book')

While Hoskins was talking privately to members of the state cabinet, the premier, as Sandford noted sadly in a draft letter, 'was telling us and our friends to wait, to wait. We quietly waited until the evening of the 19th [December 1907] when Mr Charles Hoskins told me of the proposals at his house'.[26] These proposals, which the premier presented to the Legislative Assembly on 20 December 1907, were not ungenerous to Sandford. Hoskins Bros was to pay Sandford £50 000 over ten years, with an initial instalment of £10 000. Shareholders other than Sandford himself were to receive bonds to the face value of their shares (totalling some £14 000). Hoskins guaranteed to pay off all creditors, a sum just over £26 000. As the premier, Charles Wade, said in his statement to the Legislative Assembly, 'the terms made to Mr Sandford put the latter in such a position that he would be free from anxiety, and would be financially far better off than had he remained proprietor of the works'.[27]

Better off or not, Sandford was bitterly disappointed and was critical of the way in which Charles Hoskins had allegedly undermined public support for Sandford's enterprise while planning to acquire it for himself.[28] But a consoling letter from the great bridge and hydraulic engineer Ernest de Burgh, sent to Sandford on 21 December 1907, expressed 'admiration for your perseverance', while recognizing that 'younger men will carry on the work'.[29]

A younger man did indeed take over the enterprise. Sandford was 66 years old when the blow fell, and Charles Hoskins was 10 years his junior, a man of even greater perseverance and untroubled by the internal doubts and failing memory which afflicted Sandford. But Charles Hoskins did not retire from running the Lithgow company until he was 74, while Sandford lived on in peaceful retirement in Sydney, his domestic harmony largely restored after the strains of the Lithgow years.

THE HOSKINS PERIOD 1: 1908–13

The new owners of the blast-furnace and ironworks/steelworks made little initial alteration to the blast-furnace, although there were substantial changes at the ironworks. Hoskins Bros negotiated the transfer of the state government contract from Sandford to itself with an extension of duration until the end of 1916. This gave the blast-furnace plant a secure market for the next eight years, while Hoskins Bros' Sydney pipeworks was, of course, another large consumer of the firm's Lithgow pig-iron, becoming effectively independent of overseas supplies.[30]

In December 1908 the federal bounty on locally smelted iron, for which Sandford had waited unsuccessfully, was at last passed by the Commonwealth government and came into force on 1 January 1909. The Hoskins, unlike Sandford, were already wealthy and could afford capital investment in

Lithgow as required, and, with a secure market and a handsome government subsidy, they were much better placed than Sandford to make a success in Lithgow. Events in the 1920s were to show that no one could sustain a viable iron industry in Lithgow Valley, primarily because of the expensive freight charges involved in bringing raw materials to the site and in dispatching the finished product to coastal markets, but the buoyancy in the iron and steel business which prompted Hoskins to build a second blast-furnace in 1913 was encouraging in the early years.

This general optimism was at first soured by poor labour relations in Lithgow. Sandford had been accustomed to workers' co-operatives and supportive of the separate associations formed in Lithgow by the ironworkers, coal-miners, iron-miners and iron-smelters.[31] Hoskins by contrast 'had no hesitation in opposing the growth of unionism in the iron and steel industry, showing himself an advocate of the open shop, non-union labour and day-wages', and under him 'Lithgow soon gained a name for industrial turbulence which was to outlive its history as an iron and steel town'.[32]

Hoskins believed that the Lithgow workers were overpaid in a five-year agreement negotiated by Sandford with the ironworkers in 1903, so when this agreement ran out in 1908 he reduced wages all round—and, when the ironworkers objected, closed the ironworks/steelworks on 10 July, but the blast-furnace does not seem to have been affected. The result of the trouble was the establishment in 1909 of the Iron Trades (Lithgow) Wages Board, which made its first award in March 1909, writing union preference into the terms.[33]

The trouble with all workers at Lithgow came to a head in 1911. First the iron-miners at Carcoar struck over wage levels in February, then the iron-puddlers downed tools in May, the coal-miners and the ironworkers in July and the blast-furnace workers in August. Hoskins kept the blast-furnace in operation using 'free labourers' brought in from Sydney and on 29 August 1911 there was a celebrated incident when the non-union workmen, along with Charles Hoskins' two sons, Cecil and Sid, were besieged in the Davy blowing-house at the blast-furnace, later joined by Charles himself, who ran the gauntlet of angry strikers.[34] But the blast-furnace was operating as usual the following day and non-union labour continued to function. Despite the protracted closure of the ironworks, the total pig-iron produced at the blast-furnace in 1911 was over 36000 tonnes, only 4000 tonnes less than in 1910.[35]

The year 1911 was, however, a bad one for Charles Hoskins. Following Andrew Fisher's re-election as Labor prime minister in April 1910, a Labor government was also elected in New South Wales and an ideological commitment to the nationalization of the iron and steel industry became a political reality. As a result, the government set up a royal commission on the

Charles Hoskins at the door of the Davy engine-house on 29 August 1911.
(*Hoskins Saga*)

industry in August 1911 to investigate the quality of Australian ores, the cost
of locally produced pig-iron, the desirability of the contract with Hoskins
and the capital needed to establish a new iron-producing plant. The commissioner was F. W. Paul, manager of the Steel Company of Scotland, and his
report, presented to the New South Wales parliament in October 1911, was
highly critical of Charles Hoskins, who had, after two days of interrogation,
walked out of the inquiry on 27 September.[36]

Paul was exceedingly critical of the contract price (disregarding the political function of the original concession); he also made damaging criticisms of
Hoskins' alleged dishonesty in mixing locally made steel with imported
German steel of inferior quality. The state government accordingly cancelled
the contract with Hoskins on 29 November 1911.[37]

It did not, however, proceed to nationalize the industry, because Paul had
costed the creation of an entirely new government-owned blast-furnace and
ironworks/steelworks at a realistic £1500000. The state government's enthusiasm for nationalization of Lithgow or for the establishment of a new plant
visibly cooled, although the proposition was not abandoned until after the
outbreak of the First World War in 1914.[38] The Hoskins brothers in fact
offered the government not only the entire Lithgow plant on both sites, and
their iron-mines and limestone quarries, but also their great pipe foundries at
Rhodes and Ultimo in Sydney. The *Lithgow Mercury* lobbied hard in

February and March 1914 for the state government to accept the offer, but nothing came of the negotiations.[39]

In 1911 Paul had also acted as commissioner for the Commonwealth government on the operation of the bounty for Hoskins' pig-iron and he came to similarly damaging findings. In particular, Paul found that Hoskins had claimed over £10 000 in bounty for pig-iron manufactured not from local ores but from cinders left behind by Sandford. As a result of this allegation, payment of Commonwealth bounty to Hoskins was also suspended in 1911. In fact the cinders were later proved to have been made at the blast-furnace in 1907 (that is, from local ores) and the bounty was returned to Hoskins.[40]

None the less, the favourable trading conditions which the entire iron plant at Lithgow had enjoyed in 1909 and 1910 were severely affected in 1911 and 1912. This did not inhibit the company from further massive investment in plant associated with the blast-furnace. First a decision was taken to construct coke ovens on site at Lithgow; coal from Oakey Park colliery would still be used, since this was the only part of the Lithgow seam which was reasonably well suited to coking.[41] Excavation work began late in 1910 but the bank of 80 coke ovens at the east end of the blast-furnace site, beside the railway's New Yard, was not installed until 1912 and not operative until June 1913, partly because of the general problems facing Hoskins.[42]

While the coke ovens were slowly being installed, a second blast-furnace was constructed with no less deliberate speed. Already in January 1911

The enlarged plant in 1915. (Hoskins' 'Blue Book')

Charles Hoskins had been writing to Britain seeking advice on the correct thickness of brick lining for the iron stack of the proposed new blast-furnace.[43] In a silent tribute to Sandford's ability to seek responsible advice overseas, Hoskins again used Harrison of Middlesbrough, the engineer responsible for No. 1 blast-furnace, to advise on equipment for No. 2.[44] By October 1912 Hoskins reassured the Commercial Bank manager that there was 'a large amount of the work of the Furnace erected and we have all the steel plates to complete the work',[45] but another year elapsed before the new blast-furnace was operating. It was blown in early in November 1913 with no public fanfare.[46]

Clearly Charles Hoskins was satisfied with Sandford's blast-furnace, for he built a near-replica, with rather greater capacity, casting the parts at his firm's Sydney foundry, buying another Parsons turbo-blower to supplement the one bought by Sandford, and acquiring a third turbo-blower in 1915.[47] To cope with the extra fuel required by the new blast-furnace in 1913 Hoskins decided to extend his bank of coke ovens by 15, making a total of 95.[48]

The need for iron ore and limestone also more than doubled. Prudently, Charles Hoskins had seen the likely need, since he doubted the geologists' optimistic estimates of ore at Carcoar, and as early as 1908 had acquired a lease of Tallawang near the Dunedoo–Mudgee railway. Tallawang was activated at the same time as No. 2 blast-furnace, while new sources of limestone were developed at Ben Bullen on the Mudgee line and, further out on the same railway line, at Havilah.[49]

The beginning of the First World War, therefore, saw Hoskins' iron plant poised for considerable expansion in production after a period of maximum political and economic uncertainty.

Blast-furnace coke ovens. (Hoskins' 'Blue Book', 1915)

THE HOSKINS PERIOD 2: 1914-28

The war came in the nick of time to justify the capital expenditure on the blast-furnace site. This capital had been found largely from the Commonwealth bounty which aggregated over £135000 by 1914. But on 30 June 1914 the bonus on pig-iron from Australian ores was reduced by thirty-three and a third per cent to 8 shillings a ton, and entirely removed from ironworks products. The greatly increased production of pig-iron with two blast-furnaces at work in 1914 was good, but incurred very heavy freight charges and faced cripplingly high coastal shipping rates, so that Lithgow pig-iron could barely compete in Sydney and was massively under-cut in every other capital city in Australia.[50]

Furthermore, Lithgow's monopoly on iron-smelting was about to be challenged by BHP. Taking excellent advice from America, where management and technology in the iron industry were years ahead of Britain, BHP in 1912–13 planned its Newcastle blast-furnace and steelworks, expecting to transport ore from South Australia in its own ships.[51] Newcastle, with its deep-water port and the Northern Coalfield on its doorstep, had obvious advantages, which had long been recognized, along with the similar advantages of Port Kembla on the Southern Coalfield, and the significance was not lost on Charles Hoskins and his sons Cecil and Sid.

The Newcastle plant of BHP did not open until 1915. In the meantime the problem of dumping of overseas pig-iron had been dramatically solved by warfare. Hoskins, moreover, benefited greatly by the realization of another of Sandford's pet projects, the establishment of a small arms factory in Lithgow. This had been constructed before the war, in 1911–12, but expanded rapidly when war broke out and by 1917 was employing 1300 men and women. This gave Hoskins a steady and substantial market only 3 kilometres from the blast-furnaces.[52]

Because of the war, and with the assistance of collusion over prices between Charles Hoskins and Guillaume Delprat of BHP, the Lithgow works flourished. From 1916 until 1927, with the occasional hiccup, both the blast-furnace and the steelworks returned acceptable profits.[53] A great deal of this profit was ploughed back into expansion of capacity at the steelworks. In 1923 the blast-furnace received a fifth blowing-engine, manufactured by Thompson and Co. of Castlemaine in Victoria, which at 400 tonnes was the largest engine made in Australia up to that time.[54]

The closure of the iron-mine at Carcoar in 1922 left Tallawang and Cadia, which had been opened up in 1918, as the main sources of iron ore, both some 170 kilometres from Lithgow. Ben Bullen limestone quarry was exhausted by 1922 and the extracting plant was largely moved to Excelsior, on the Mudgee line.[55] But Charles Hoskins' prescience had also led him to acquire for the company leases at Marulan, 'simply a mountain of limestone', and Marulan, once the source of Fitzroy flux, was to be the chief source of supply for Port Kembla.[56]

It is quite clear that the decision to move from Lithgow to Port Kembla had been made soon after the First World War ended. The ideal of finding in one area the combination of viable iron ore, coking coal and limestone had proved unattainable in Australia. The attractiveness of sea transport for heavy raw materials had been well understood by the Tasmanian blast-furnace entrepreneurs of the 1870s, who looked across Bass Strait to Newcastle for the coal which they lacked. BHP was showing from 1915 onwards that it was economic to bring iron ore by their own vessels from South Australia to Newcastle. Hoskins was already using Southern Coalfield coal for coke in preference to the Western Coalfield product and had bought a coal-mine at Wongawilli near Dapto, where in 1917 he built coke ovens to supply Lithgow. By 1924 there were 80 coke ovens in operation, producing about 2000 tonnes a week. A further 40 ovens were added in 1927.[57]

Hoskins also bought land in Port Kembla eminently suitable for a blast-furnace and steelworks. In 1923, in his director's report to what was now Hoskins Iron & Steel Co. Ltd, Charles said roundly that 'for the present we suggest we make every endeavour to have the railway (from Port Kembla to Moss Vale) constructed, and when it is a certainty *and not before* we make arrangements to erect our Blast Furnace at "Port Kembla"'.[58] The construction of this railway would link the Illawarra coast with the main south line, giving better access not only to inland markets but also to Marulan limestone.

The state parliamentary committee on public works heard evidence about the proposed 60 kilometres of new railway in March 1923. Charles Hoskins gave evidence that 'as soon as they knew the line would be started his firm intended to establish works at Port Kembla', and said that 'to my mind Port Kembla is the finest place in Australia for a steel works'.[59] In December 1923 the committee recommended the construction of the railway—and over the next few years it was built. It was not, however, fully operational until 1932. Hoskins Iron & Steel did not keep to Charles Hoskins' private intent of waiting for completion but agreed in the Moss Vale to Port Kembla Ratification Act of 1927 to commence the new iron complex concurrently with work on the connecting railway to Moss Vale.[60]

The construction of the Port Kembla works began in January 1927 and the American blast-furnace chosen by Sid Hoskins was lit in August 1928, using iron ore bought from BHP, coke from Wongawilli and limestone from Marulan.[61] Charles Hoskins did not live to see any of the new plant, for he had died in February 1926.[62]

The consequences for Lithgow were, of course, catastrophic. While Port Kembla was still in the planning and building stage, Lithgow was kept going to produce the maximum profit. A second-hand Ferranti generator was installed in a new engine-house at the blast-furnace in 1925[63] and the Steelworks Colliery shaft was sunk in 1926.[64] But Charles Hoskins' *obiter dictum* of January 1925 that 'as little money as possible be expended at Lithgow and as much money as is available be expended at "Port Kembla"'[65] was loyally followed by his son Cecil.

In November 1928, three months after the Port Kembla blast-furnace was blown in, the two blast-furnaces at Lithgow ceased production. Although the last employees at the steelworks were dismissed only on 12 January 1932,[66] the blast-furnace site had been abandoned at the end of 1928 to the demolishers and Lithgow was left, drained of its premier industry, to face the Depression of the 1930s.

What of Sandford?

Sandford's anxieties had been resolved for him. His doubts about whether to live in Sydney or at Eskroy were dissolved by the loss of Eskroy; his various schemes for separating from Mrs Caroline Sandford (by living in Sydney while she lived in Lithgow; or by living in Lithgow while she lived in Sydney; or by sending her and the children to Philadelphia or Birmingham, Alabama; or by himself wintering in England)[67] all became unnecessary as he withdrew to Darling Point in Sydney and rechristened the house Torrington, after his birthplace.[68]

Finally, he found some measure of peace in running an orchard in Castle Hill at the eponymous Sandford Glen.[69] The wheel came full cycle from Torrington in Devon to Torrington in Darling Point and then to Sandford Glen. In their own ways, both he and his stay-at-home brother Robert displayed remarkable entrepreneurial ambitions, but premature ageing, the lack of ruthless single-mindedness and a measure of sheer bad luck turned the brothers into interesting failures. William approached heroic failure. A benevolent capitalist, remarkably sympathetic to socialism, genuinely concerned to alleviate the lot of the Lithgow worker, William Sandford is a striking contrast to his successor, Charles Hoskins. Hoskins had his own brand of heroism in the face of the 1908 and 1911 strikes at Lithgow, but Sandford's was a gentler brand. The engineer Ernest de Burgh wrote to Sandford in December 1907:

> I can assure you that no one in this state has had this matter of the establishment of the Iron & Steel industry closer at heart than I have had—nor has anyone a greater admiration for the pluck and perseverance with which you followed your purpose . . . You have done what you started to do; younger men will carry on the work, but your name will always be associated with it and it must be a pleasure to you to know that the admiration for your perseverance which I have ventured to express is felt by all classes in the State.[70]

Without Sandford there would have been no iron-making industry in New South Wales before the First World War. His achievement, despite many failings of character and deficiencies in technical training, was at the cost of immense personal unhappiness because of the strains endured between the 1890s and 1907. But the achievement was a great one and the plant which he created was maintained by the Hoskins brothers for another 20 years. Sandford said in 1920: 'Hoskins have carried out my plans, and they kept on all the staff I had, and I do say that I had the ability to employ ability.'[71] It was not an empty boast.

CHAPTER EIGHT

LITHGOW TODAY

At the time of writing, the Lithgow blast-furnace site is a public park, con-served and landscaped by the Greater Lithgow City Council as part of the 1988 Bicentennial programme. The site is now so tidy that it is difficult to appreciate that it once dominated the town with its noise, heat and fumes, casting a permanent cloud of smoke over the city centre. It was never liked by the people of Lithgow, for the working conditions were always harsh and the struggle to improve them a source of conflict.[1] Worst of all, just when more decent conditions had been created, the plant was abruptly shut down. The removal of the iron industry to Port Kembla came almost without notice, though rumours had circulated, as Charles Hoskins had been at pains to deny that everything would be moved.[2] It is possible that he himself intended to maintain some plant at Lithgow, but his death coincided with the closure of the works and his heirs took a different course.

The closure of the blast-furnace signalled the failure of Lithgow as an industrial centre. The place once acclaimed as a new Pittsburgh, ideally located to be the capital of the new Commonwealth of Australia,[3] had by

General view of Lithgow in 1924, showing the blast-furnaces at centre with the town at left and the steelworks at right. Railway roundhouse in foreground. (From a watercolour by Albert Collins, ML, Small Picture File)

123

1928 lost all claims to industrial pre-eminence. The move to Port Kembla took with it more than men and machines. It took away many skilled workers and managers, better-paid people whose families were consumers of both goods and services. There was thus an immediate financial effect on local businesses, compounded by the loss of wages suffered by the less-skilled workers, who then fell victim to the Depression of the 1930s. Lithgow survived through determination and self-help, but its tremendous bitterness at the closure of the iron industry has powerfully affected its attitude to the industrial heritage.

The site itself was stripped of any reusable machinery and most of the iron fabric scrapped, leaving behind only the more solid foundations. Half-hearted attempts to demolish the buildings were, fortunately, not entirely successful. The furnace remained in meaningless isolation, surrounded by heaps of its own slag and ashes, to which, over many years, were added dumps of unrelated industrial machinery and gravel. In Lithgow's view the site was a humiliating eyesore, which should be entirely destroyed. Its value as a memorial to two generations of ironworkers was cancelled out by the permanent reminder of abandonment.

The 1988 landscaping has stressed picturesque values by surrounding the surviving remains with neat walks and rows of exotic trees. The slag dump between Inch Street and the blast-furnaces has been totally removed and the site opened for redevelopment. Visitors can walk around the industrial remains, which are quite visible, though cordoned-off for safety reasons. Signs identify the various structures, but there are no interpretive panels and it is difficult to understand either the purpose of the site or its relation to the wider Lithgow context.

The most noticeable feature is Sandford's monumental engine-house, its tower almost a romantic ruin. When first built, however, it was a refined industrial building with high arches on all four sides, framing superimposed pairs of arched windows, separated by round portholes. The windows were glazed, allowing daylight to flood into the engine-house, illuminating the superb vertical blower which entirely filled the building. This Davy engine had been imported from Britain, carried in sections from Sydney on specially altered railway trucks and assembled on-site over a six-week period. It was a major showpiece and was accordingly displayed in a setting which almost belied its industrial function: the interior walls had at their base a deep band of white tiling edged in dark red paint; the arched windows were made up of small square panes; the great vertical engine with two fly-wheels sat atop a foundation block concealed below a wooden floor. Today the floor has gone, and this massive foundation can be seen to be over 2 metres deep. The bolts which held down the engine are still in position, but are sheared off where they connected with it. The life of the machinery has left its traces in thick

Sandford's plant late in 1907, showing the Davy engine-house at left, with pump house in front and boiler house at rear. The pig-beds are in the foreground, No.1 furnace in the centre, with three stoves and its chimney behind it, and to its right the steam-hoist for loading the charge. At the extreme right are the elevated rail line and 'truck drop' over the materials storage bins. (ML, Government Printer 3315)

Davy engine in 1907. (ML, Government Printer 3316)

deposits of black sludge on the foundation block, on parts of the interior and on the outer western wall. Folk-memory has caused some anonymous graffi-tist to inscribe the name of the 1980s rock group Iron Maiden on the wall facing the space where once stood the phallic blower.

The Davy engine was connected on the south side by a broad open arch-way to a second engine-house, which held a reclining blower, a state-of-the-art Parsons turbine. This house, too, had arched windows with square panes, tiled and painted walls and a wooden floor, even though the engine was an afterthought, not ordered till midway through the main construction in 1906. Neither engine nor house has survived, but evocative traces have been left in the form of large engine foundations and a particularly telling outline on the Davy house's south wall. This outline shows two roof lines, the origi-nal one of 1906, below which the wall is painted white, and above it the 1913 addition of a glazed clerestory, this one unpainted. It is also evident that the Parsons house was an afterthought, for the roof line cuts across the port-holes of the Davy house's south wall: these have not been pierced for glazing but have been bricked as decorative roundels.

Both the vertical and the horizontal blowers were powered by the steam from a set of four Babcock & Wilcox boilers, which were imported from England in what must surely be a record time, as two of them arrived in Sydney on 27 April 1906, having been ordered less than two months previ-ously on 2 March. The remaining pair arrived in Sydney on 8 June. These boilers were south-west of the engine-houses in a shed, which was extended in 1910 and 1913 to house three more pairs. In contrast to the engine-houses, this shed seems to have been quite insubstantial, its roof held up on old iron

Parsons turbine in 1907. (ML, Government Printer 3317)

tram-rails set vertically in concrete to act as columns. Their stumps can still be seen. The boilers were fired with local coal, stored on a concrete floor along the Davy house's west wall, and were essentially water-tubes suspended in the hot gases of the coal fire.

The water for the boilers came from a well on the east side of the Davy house and was pumped up to a large rectangular iron water-tank, which doubled as the roof of the engine-house. Water could be recirculated by condensing any waste steam back into water in a cooling pond just beside the well. The whole arrangement was an ingenious one, and economical of space. The pump house was built on to the Davy house and has left the ghost of its roof line on that house's west wall, and also a well-preserved set of pits and red-painted footings, on which once stood the steam-operated pumps. The well is visible just outside, as a low, circular brick wall, and the cooling pond to its east has been exposed by clearing during the Bicentennial conservation programme.

The cooling pond is a particularly evocative remnant, not of its industrial operation, but of industrial unrest, for it was here that 'blackleg workers' were harassed during the great strike of 1911–12. In those nine months from 28 August 1911 to 18 April 1912 the blast-furnace was kept alight, though it is not clear whether it actually produced much iron, or was simply charged with small quantities of fuel. Non-union labour was brought in to keep it going, much to the resentment of the normal workforce, which vented its anger by throwing the new workers' personal things into the cooling pond, a small but effective measure at a time when casual labour was extremely poorly paid and could ill afford to lose any possessions.

Although the engine-house dominates the site today, it was in its time

Cooling pond during the 1911–12 strike. (Eskbank House, Lithgow, 7061.77)

127

Construction site on 9 September 1906, from the north, showing the I-columns of the furnace at centre, with stoves, chimney and steam-hoist at right and Davy engine-house at left. The boiler chimneys are in the background. Compare this with the finished plant, on p. 112. (ML, PXA149)

only one component of a much larger complex, of which only the foundations now survive. The whole layout was planned by Sandford, though he built only the first half, and its construction was photographed at monthly intervals between May 1906 and March 1907 by a local photographer, Austin Cockerton. This superb record is particularly meaningful since it shows the creation of precisely those foundations which have survived and also gives an insight into working conditions at the time. In less than a year, with no earth-moving equipment and only one lifting-crane, the workmen built the engine- and boiler-houses, the furnace and three of its four stoves, the pig-beds, the materials bunkers and a steam-hoist. The speed of construction was remarkable, but the work was of such good quality that all the foundations have survived in good shape. The remains now on site can be matched with the construction photographs in a remarkably precise way.

The first job was to cut back the western slope of Coal Stage Hill to create a level area on which the plant could be erected. Two hundred and thirty men with 48 horses and drays removed 35 000 cubic yards of earth in about three weeks. The working area was 10 metres lower than the original surface and is a long strip approximately 200 metres long and 100 metres wide, sloping gently downwards towards the railway line which runs along its south-

Construction site on 9 September 1906, from the south. (ML, PXA149)

ern edge. The artificially cut hill still marks the north-eastern edge of the site, though its original surface is now buried under later deposits of ash and slag.

The entire working level was covered with concrete and a railway system was laid out, intended to bring in building materials in the first instance and for later permanent use, for the supply of raw materials to the furnace and the delivery of smelted iron back to the main railway line. The line ran along the back of the furnace stoves, which were built atop a level platform about 65 metres long, 20 metres wide and raised ten metres above the adjacent ground surface. The construction of this entire section can be followed month by month in the 1906 photographs.

The Cowper stoves were very large, vertical iron containers, about seven metres in diameter, twenty-four metres high and filled with a chequerwork of perforated bricks through which hot air or gases circulated, until the bricks reached a heat of 900 degrees C. At this point the air which blasted into the furnace was passed through the stove for pre-heating. As each stove reached the requisite temperature the heating gases were switched to the next, and so on in sequence. The gases were recycled from the exhaust of the blast-furnace and, after circulating through the stoves, were emitted through a high chimney stack, forming the distinctive cloud over Lithgow.

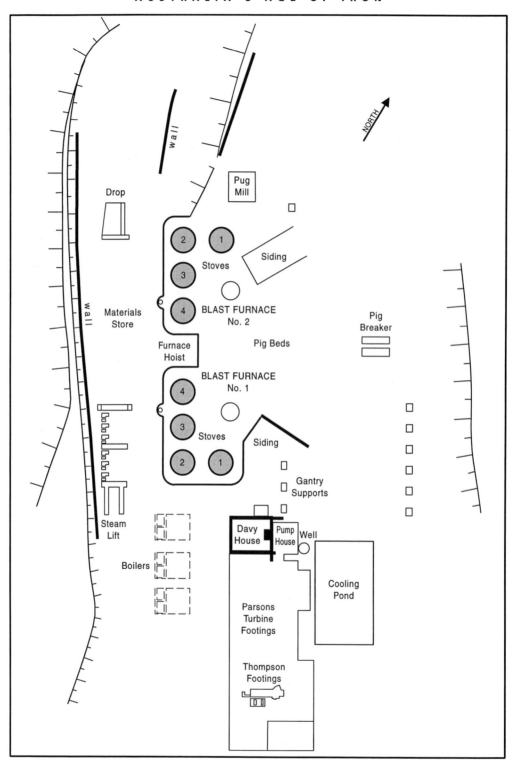

Plan of the remains on the blast-furnace site. (University of Sydney Cartography, from plan by J. Gibson, in Cremin and Jack, 1986, 5.1)

Though Sandford laid the foundations for four stoves, he actually built only three, which were completed between May and November 1906, using metal plates fabricated at the ironworks but imported chequer bricks. The Hoskins completed the fourth stove (No. 1) in 1911–12 and added a second set of four to service their new blast-furnace in 1913. While Sandford's chimney stack was of brick, 46 metres high, with the inscription 'W S 1906' painted towards the top, the Hoskins' chimney stack was of brick-lined steel and somewhat higher. In all other respects the appearance of the second set of stoves and stack was very similar to that of 1906, though construction took twice as long, from June 1911 to August 1913.

The platform on which the stoves and furnaces sat is still visible today, edged by a fine brick revetment wall pierced by arches which are accessways to the flues for cleaning the stoves. The first set of stoves apparently used to be cleaned by firing a small cannon inside one of these flues: this dislodged the dust clogging the inside, but also damaged the brick arches.[4] However, they have survived quite well, as have the bases of the two chimney stacks, projecting outwards from the brick platform wall. The concrete bases for the metal stoves are in good condition and three of the bottom plates for the stoves still exist, flat octagonal plates made up of 25 cast-iron sheets riveted together in cobweb pattern. Two have been moved and partly cut up, but one is still in its original location at the northernmost end of the bank. The brick cladding has been partly stripped off, which usefully exposes the concrete base. The stoves are lined up in two sets of three with the fourth stove for each furnace sited at a right angle, north and south of the main set. The base of the No. 1 stove, the one closest to the Davy engine-house, has been exposed by the 1988 clearance and the details of construction are quite clear even from a distance.

General view of the blast-furnace site in 1992, from the same viewpoint as in the photo on p. 112. (A. Cremin)

The two blast-furnaces were lined up side by side between the pair of No. 1 stoves, facing eastwards on to the pig-beds. Their remains are at first rather disappointing, showing up mostly as hollow brick circles, quite overwhelmed by the spectacular bosh skull of No. 2 furnace which lies between them. Closer inspection, however, reveals a number of interesting details which can be matched up with the construction photographs. The Hoskins seem to have simply replicated the foundations of Sandford's furnace and the structural details appear identical. In each instance the furnace was a large iron container, imported in the case of No. 1 furnace, locally made in the case of No. 2 furnace. It sat on iron columns of I-shaped sections, which were 7 metres high, the furnace itself being the same height as the stoves, 24 metres. The furnaces had a fire-brick lining, a little over one metre thick, and the hearth was a hollow brick column which sat on a concrete pedestal. The concrete and brick bases still survive though they are not now easy to see.

The base of No. 2 furnace is the better-preserved, being still edged with the heavy metal staves of its cooling jacket. A gap in the ring of staves shows the location of the slag notch through which molten slag once flowed. All around the furnace are the remains of the I-columns cut off just above the

The authors recording the bosh skull, with the Davy engine-house in the background. (R. de Berquelle, 1986)

base when the furnace itself was removed for scrap in 1929. One has been crushed by the dense metallic mass of the bosh skull, which must have fallen on it during demolition. The skull, a congealed mass of slag and iron, was probably formed because the furnace was shut down abruptly with molten metal still inside it. It was not worth removing and has remained as a strikingly sculptural artefact visually dominating the furnace platform. Between the skull and the engine-house area is the base of No. 1 furnace, a brick column, reinforced with iron bands, which once supported the hearth of the furnace, now heavily encrusted with a layer of slag and iron skull. Most of its metalwork has been removed and the brick column is surrounded by a robber trench dug to extract the iron jacket, staves and columns which matched those still surviving on No. 2 furnace.

The furnaces when full contained about 350 tonnes of combined fuel, iron ore and flux. These materials were loaded from the top, while the hot blast was forced through the base of the furnace. There were thus four zones in the furnace: at the very base the combustion zone, where the hot air reacted with the fuel to create an intense heat, over 1600 degrees C; above that the melting or fusion zone, where the reactions between ore, fuel and flux effectively took place; above that again the heat absorption zone, where the various materials were continuously affected by the intense heat from below; and above that again the initial reduction zone, where oxygen was driven from the iron oxide ore, by chemically combining with the carbon monoxide from the burning coke to produce carbon dioxide, which was then expelled in the gas driven out of the furnace through the gas catchers to heat the stoves. As the iron melted it sank into the rising gas and fuel, from which it picked up some impurities, which had to be removed later on, during the steel-making process.

Having sunk to the very bottom of the bosh the molten iron flowed through its tap notch on to the sand-covered pig-beds and was directed by the workers into comb-like channels, traditionally nicknamed the 'sow and pigs'. Originally the pigs were broken off by hand, by striking one blow at the junction of sow and pig, but late in the life of the plant a mechanical system was installed which considerably reduced the labour required. A row of 24 pigs, weighing about two tonnes, was lifted by crane and brought to the pig-breaking machine, north of the pig-beds.

The pig-beds are really the most important part of any iron-making site, since making the pigs is the only purpose of all the other operations, but paradoxically they are the least striking part of the Lithgow remains, as they now consist only of an overgrown area sloping gently eastwards from the furnaces. The area has deliberately not been cleared, so as to preserve any remains of the casting-sand which might have survived. When the plant was working, fresh sand, brought in from Perthville, near Bathurst, would be laid down as needed; as the sand came into contact with the burning iron it formed a crust down which the iron could flow without impediment. However, if the sand got wet, the iron boiled the water and soaked down with it into the sand, creating a major blockage, as well as ruining the iron, which had to be discarded. Nevertheless, the pig-beds at Lithgow, as at Redbill Point, were not normally covered, except in the immediate vicinity of the tap hole, where there was a small awning. The pig-bed workers, wearing thick wooden clogs, would walk along the beds, with long-handled iron cutters, semicircular cast-iron plates with bevelled edges, which could stop the flow of iron and direct it into the appropriate channel. As the furnace was tapped the melted iron was let flow to the far end of the pig-bed and then progressively filled the pig-channels back towards the furnace.

Supply and delivery were of crucial importance to the operation of the site. Any given amount of iron ore requires approximately 50 per cent of its volume in fuel (coke) and 30 per cent in flux (limestone). These raw materials had to be on hand in large quantities and their storage and loading took up about one-third of the total working area. They were kept in heaps, separated by tall vertical wooden or brick walls, forming a long set of bunkers, parallel to the furnace area. Here, too, Sandford's arrangements were ingenious and space-saving. The raw materials were delivered by rail in hoppers, which were loaded on to a steam-lift and then on to an elevated railway, which ran along the top of the set of bunkers, bringing the hoppers to the appropriate bin. The hoppers opened, discharged their contents and were run on to the north end of the bins. There they were dropped by a system of counter-weights back on to the railway line to start loading once more. Most of the bunker walls were made of timber, but to minimize the risk of fire the coke-bin walls, at the southern end, were made of brick, as was the northernmost wall, which supported the 'truck drop' system of counterweights. The brick walls still stand, and the 'drop pit' for the empty hoppers has been cleared. Parallel to the line of bins, clearance has also exposed two long concrete walls. They are the supports for a set of rails on which ran a travelling crane, which dumped reserve material into stockpiles—a later feature of the site, probably built during the First World War, when Lithgow's furnace was working at full blast, using up to 15 000 tonnes of raw material a week.

In Sandford's time, loading the raw materials into the furnace was labour-intensive and very dangerous. Raw materials were manually loaded into barrows which were wheeled over to the back of the furnace complex, which man and barrow ascended in a steam-hoist. The top of the hoist was connected by a gangway to the top of the furnace and each man had to wheel his barrow to the edge of the furnace where he tipped in his load, receiving the full impact of the heat. The Hoskins improved on this system by adding mechanical tippers to the top of each of the furnaces.[5]

The furnaces melted not only the iron ore, but also the coke fuel and the limestone flux, which extracted impurities from the ore. Spent coke and flux combine together to form the slag, which in its molten state flowed out of the furnaces through the 'slag notch' and was collected in slag ladles, which ran on a railway system to the dumps. Each of the Lithgow furnaces had its slag railway, and part of the No. 1 system has been exposed by clearance: it is now visible as a levelled area between the pig-beds and the Davy engine-house, bounded by the brick-clad concrete of the No. 1 stove base and of the pig-bed base. The corresponding system for No. 2 furnace is rather different, as it was dug quite deep into the ground and has tended to fill with water. The slag siding was also used for the rail system which carried the hot-metal cars to the steelworks. This rail system was a typically bold and risky Hoskins innovation, for it involved bringing the ladles, each holding 30 tonnes of white-hot molten metal, directly over Inch Street in what must have been a highly dramatic manner.

Slag cools into a quite bulky but lightweight substance which can be used for road metal or fill. It was efficiently recycled at Lithgow to build up ground for the blast-furnace-to-steelworks rail link and a wall of stratified slag can be seen at the south-west of the site, alongside the current visitor-access track. There was until quite recently a lunar graveyard of slag directly behind the houses on Inch Street, but regrettably most of this has now been removed, taking with it a vivid reminder of the furnaces' operations, for it included not only piles of ash and slag but also many remains of 'tyre scrap', which was one of Lithgow's more picturesque cost-cutting devices. Discarded iron railway tyres were used to pick up slag or skull that might have formed, for instance, in a wet pig-bed; the tyre was half-embedded into the still-liquid material which solidified around it. The projecting part of the tyre was then easily scooped up by a crane and the whole thing carried over to the dump.

Sandford's plant was effectively built in just under a year. The furnace was blown in at the end of April, and officially opened by the Premier of New South Wales on 13 May 1907. This was a tremendous ceremony attended by scores of people, who are seen crowding all around the pig-beds, and even on the high loading-gangway in the memorial photograph. Other photographs of this date show Sandford and his managers posing in front of the first stacks of pig-iron and at the base of the furnace. Another picture, of formally dressed men on the steps of the Parsons turbo-house, has the caption 'these *are* the men that made the first Pig iron in Australia'. The statement is technically true if we take 'Australia' to refer to the political entity created in 1901, but it is misleading, since iron had, of course, been smelted in the country before.

The fine-sounding half-truths are regrettably characteristic of Sandford's nationalist rhetoric and generally of the iron industry in those early days. In later years the Hoskins would denigrate Sandford's achievements, claiming, for instance, to have virtually remodelled the plant, while in reality they carried out the second half of Sandford's original plan, building a second furnace complex with accompanying engine-houses. They did not mechanize pig-breaking until 1916, nor install electricity until 1925.

The Hoskins' improvements were concerned not so much with the technology of the blast-furnace operations as with rationalizing the supply system. In 1911 a large water reservoir was excavated on the east of Coal Stage Hill and named Lake Pillans, in unsubtle homage to the then lord mayor. To its east, alongside the railway line, construction started on a bank of 80 coke ovens, built of literally millions of local bricks. A new coal-mine, the Steelworks mine, was opened in 1912, and in 1913 the private rail line bridged Inch Street, and carried molten iron directly to the works. In this way iron-making became far more integrated into the now gigantic Hoskins operation and also a far more visible part of Lithgow's life.

While Sandford was essentially a late nineteenth-century paternalist, whose grasp of economics was always shaky, the Hoskins were firm capitalists, prepared to cut labour costs by streamlining operations and by introducing more mechanization, however frugally. They invested heavily in new machinery but spent little on building stock, which was modern, lightweight, easily erected and dismantled. As a result no walls now stand of the three new engine-houses built in the decade 1913–23, to the south of the Davy house. There are, however, extensive remains of the foundations of the new engines at the entrance to the site, immediately beside the visitors' carpark.

The new machines were quite spectacular: two more Parsons turbo-blowers, imported from England in 1913 and 1916, and a Thompson engine, specially cast in Victoria and installed in 1923. The 1913 Parsons was much the same as Sandford's and sat in an extension of the 1906 house. It was powered by a second set of Babcock & Wilcox boilers, to the same specifications as Sandford's, and mounted in the enlarged boiler house. In contrast, the 1916 Parsons had double the capacity and was housed along with an electric generator in a long building, of which the concrete floor and very substantial concrete footings for the engine and the generator still exist. The 1923 engine was an important engineering achievement, being the first engine of its size ever built in Australia, an enormous horizontal cross-compound engine, weighing over 400 tonnes, designed and built by Thompsons of Castlemaine, Victoria. It was appropriately housed at the southern end of the engine-houses complex. The bases of its structural columns survive as metal plates set into the concrete foundations and its service pit is the very first feature seen by today's visitors.

The wartime years of 1914–16 had kept the blast-furnace busy and midway through the war a mechanical pig-breaker was constructed, which overcame some of the manpower problems experienced by most industries in those years. Considerable physical strength was required to break the pigs off their sow by hand, though an experienced man could do it with one blow. The effort required can be visualized by looking at the size and solidity of the foundations for the pig-breaker, a pair of solid brick structures, 9 metres long, 2 metres high and 1.8 metres wide. They are set east of the pig-beds from which the pigs were transported by a 5-tonne crane, which travelled along a pair of gantries, 38 metres apart. The gantries' square concrete footings survive in two parallel lines, one running just east of the furnace remains, over the pig-beds, one behind the pig-breaker at the foot of the artificial scarp of Coal Stage Hill.

After the war, George Hoskins, the older brother, left the firm, and in 1920 the G. & C. Hoskins company became Hoskins Iron & Steel, later to be known as Australian Iron & Steel. Developments after this time were ever larger, but also more unsatisfactory, as it became clear that Lithgow was simply not able to compete with the BHP works at Newcastle. Charles Hoskins was starting to consider reorganizing on a really large scale and eventually took the momentous decision to begin a new operation in Port Kembla, where South Australian iron ore could be smelted with Illawarra coke and Marulan limestone. Despite this forward planning, Hoskins seems to have wanted to retain some presence in Lithgow, for throughout 1925 there was discussion about building a new set of 40 regenerative coke ovens.[6] Presumably these were intended to replace the set of 80 ovens built in 1911–12, even though it must have been clear that Lithgow coal was not really suitable for coking. The 1911–12 ovens had been a disaster right from the start, as their construction had been delayed by strikes and by financial problems. They took over two and a half years to complete, from November 1910 to August 1913, and worked only sporadically from 1914 to 1916.[7]

As so often with industrial archaeology, the least successful leaves the most enduring monument and the Hoskins coke ovens are still remarkably well-preserved, largely because they are almost invisible under a cover of brambles which occupies a triangular section of ground between the railway line and the eastern end of Inch Street. The loading devices which stood close to the railway line have been quite unnecessarily vandalized by their owners since the 1980s, which has destroyed part of the industrial context. Nevertheless, it is still possible to see the façade of the ovens: a fine brick wall, pierced with arched openings, running parallel to the railway line, as shown in the official photographs of the Hoskins Blue and Black Books.

The families of the workers were offered housing on property acquired by Sandford from Rutherford as part of the ironworks purchase. Both Sandford

The coke ovens in 1992. (R.Ian Jack)

and the Hoskins released parcels of this land for lease or sale, so that there was once almost a separate ironworkers' village, stretching from Inch Street to the former ironworks site (now the Margery Jackson sportsground). Sandford is commemorated by Sandford Street, the Hoskins by Hoskins Avenue.

The Hoskins family also commemorated itself with three buildings of exceptional quality, donated to the people of Lithgow. The Hoskins Memorial Church on Mort Street, a simple Gothic structure, is a double memorial, commemorating not only the Hoskins family, but also the two sons of its landscape designer, Paul Sorensen, who built into the grounds a monument in the form of a Danish dolmen. The church was completed in 1928, its parish hall having been opened in 1924. Charles Hoskins is also commemorated in the Charles Hoskins Memorial Literary Institute, which is said to have then included a library with many thousands of volumes, lecture rooms, a reading room, a concert hall and a gymnasium. It still serves as the Lithgow City Library and in its size and ambitions was indeed a fitting memorial to a great ironmaster.

The Institute was opened in December 1927 by Thomas Bavin, Premier of New South Wales, who said of Charles Hoskins that 'he would be remembered as a great "captain of industry", as a man who played an important part in building up what was the most important industry of the Commonwealth, and as a man of indomitable pluck, enterprise and perseverance'.[8] All of these qualities had been present in varying degrees in Australia's iron-makers in the nineteenth century and in Sandford in the twentieth, but Charles Hoskins and his BHP counterpart, Essington Lewis, were thinking and building on such a different scale from their predecessors that their achievement was to be incommensurably greater.

CONCLUSION

'The history of [New South Wales] is littered over with the ruins of heroic efforts made by other brave men to do what the Hoskins have done; but from the beginning right down to Mr Sandford's heroic attempt, all ended in ignominious failure.'[1] At Eskbank in about 1884 James Rutherford 'blew the [blast-furnace] down and melted up the ironwork so that he might not be tempted to work it again'.[2] In Tasmania during the 1870s five companies failed within a few months or, at best, a few years: iron ore 'of extraordinary richness'[3] used at Redbill Point proved to be irregularly contaminated with chromium; Algernon Swift's death was untimely, and with him died the Tamar Hematite Iron Company; Ilfracombe smelter declined to smelt; and the siting of the Derwent blast-furnace, beside its market in Hobart, but far away from all its raw materials, was too progressive for its potential backers.[4]

In South Australia, the luckless blast-furnace manager at Mount Jagged attributed a series of disastrous failures 'to a great extent to our having placed too much confidence in the furnace-keepers',[5] but Dubois could not have known that the titanium in the ore would have been a problem to the best furnace-keepers anywhere.

At Lal Lal in Victoria the second, quite effective, furnace on a well-designed, contoured site was on the brink of greater success in 1884 after the opening of its tramway to the main railway. But the dramatic decline in the cost of imported pig-iron had its effect almost at once and the 5 kilometres of tramway were in use for only 14 weeks.

The most long-lived of the colonial blast-furnaces, at Mittagong, was dogged by technical problems and inadequately skilled management. The free-trade policies of New South Wales governments made Fitzroy especially susceptible to shifts in British iron production, and already in 1877, after the price of imported pig-iron had reached its peak, Fitzroy iron, like Lal Lal iron in 1884, cost more to produce than the retail price of British imports.

The concentration of Australian iron-smelting in the five years 1873 to 1877 is very striking: only Fitzroy is earlier and only Lal Lal and Eskbank survived into the 1880s. A simple impetus was given to local entrepreneurs and some British investors by the unlegislated protectionism of the high prices and simultaneous scarcity of British export iron. The optimism was widespread and led to a number of abortive enterprises other than those discussed in detail in this book.

In 1874 the *Border Post*, an Albury newspaper, proclaimed the opening of Bogolong iron-mines near Yass by Albury investors; after employing seven men for the latter part of 1873 and beyond, a small smelting furnace was erected which produced a small quantity of iron on 31 March 1874 and again on 20 May, 'equal in quality to that of the best Swedish'. The Bogolong Iron Mining Company did not prosper, the experiment failed, and, contrary to local hopes in both Yass and Albury, Bogolong iron did not 'play an important part in the great iron market of the world'. The perspective of Australian optimists in the 1870s is nowhere more touchingly expressed than in the Albury journalist's introduction to the Bogolong story: 'The recent scarcity of iron in the English markets, and the high prices charged by iron masters, must be greatly influenced by the recent discoveries of iron ore throughout the colony of New South Wales.'[6] The ironstone of Bogolong did not greatly influence the English market or its pricing, but it is revealing that local pride should express the interaction in this unexpected way.

The Albury newspaper was an unsophisticated vehicle for a broader sentiment. The 1870s were to iron what the 1850s had been to gold: of course the immediate results of the iron craze were tiny compared to those of the gold-rushes, but for the first time in 1873 and beyond prospectors were sniffing out iron deposits and assessing furnace fuel in a small imitation of the panning for alluvial gold and assaying of auriferous quartz. The *Illustrated Sydney News* ran a series on 'the underground permanent wealth of New South Wales' in 1873 and included iron.[7] The *Sydney Morning Herald* had run articles on iron in 1865 and 1868, but these were both in a series entitled 'the manufacturing industries of New South Wales'[8]: Fitzroy was well described on 27 and 30 July 1868, but the other articles were devoted to the major foundries, such as Peter Nicol Russell's. The exploratory zeal of the *Illustrated Sydney News* in 1873 is a striking and characteristic contrast.

> Starting from Wallerawang [near Lithgow], we followed up the Piper Flat Creek, on a gently-rising road, for about four miles, when we arrived at the destined site for the works of the Great Western Iron and Coal Company. Leaving our horses, we walked over to the opposite hills, crossing a rivulet of the purest ever-running water. Turning up a gully, where it is proposed to place the blast furnace—*and no place could command more facilities* [our emphasis]—we ascended to the top seam of coal [already mined] . . . Being on the face of so high a hill, this coal can be run at once, by gravitation, into the furnaces as required.

The iron deposit lay six kilometres away to the south-west across Piper's Flat Creek near the headwaters of a tributary, still known as Irondale Creek; and midway there was a limestone quarry. 'By the fortunate juxtaposition of our coal, iron, lime, with abundance of fire-clay, iron may be manufactured on this fine property at a lower cost than at any other place we have ever seen or heard of; and then [the final, clinching argument] may even be carried to the railway at Wallerawang by gravitation.'[9] The blast-furnace was never built, although the ironstone was used at Rutherford's plant at Eskbank and later by Sandford.

The phrase 'and no place could command more facilities' is, however, a clarion declaration of the thinking behind site selection throughout the colonies. There was, for cogent enough reasons, a preoccupation with the area which had, by geological accident, deposits of ore, of coal and of flux with the minimum of transportation expenses. If there was no coal, as in the Tamar Valley, or no suitable coal, as at Lal Lal, then charcoal might be an acceptable local alternative, as it was in America throughout the nineteenth century.[10] The ideal conjunction of fuel, flux and ore of suitable and compatible quality never in fact occurred. The blast-furnaces at Bogolong, Swift's Jetty and Ilfracombe came closest to enjoying a suitable conjunction, but all were very short-lived for other reasons. Charcoal was quite expensive, for charcoal-burners enjoyed high incomes in their isolated self-employment,[11] but could produce good quality iron: the Swedish example was often cited by Australian ironmasters. None the less, the future lay with coke and with the higher furnaces which coke made regularly possible. And the persistent failure of iron ore to be found adjacent to good coking coal was a recurrent complaint—at Lithgow, in particular, which, for all its geological wealth, had no coal seams which could reliably support the blast-furnace with coke. There were ovens at Oakey Park and at New Vale, coking the coal beside the pit-head, but only when coal was brought by train from the Illawarra coalfield to Hoskins' own ovens near the blast-furnace was coke of satisfactory quality actually produced in Lithgow.

It is easy to see in hindsight that the future lay not with inland sites like Lithgow but with coastal works on deep-water anchorages supplied by coastal shipping, with iron ore from far away but using local coking coal and limestone. The creation and marketing of the finished product were no longer dependent on railway freight concessions. Fitzroy, Lal Lal and Mount Jagged lay, like Lithgow, inconveniently far from really extensive markets and even between Lal Lal and its local foundry market in Ballarat transport remained slow and clumsy until Lal Lal's time had already passed. The first attempts to use the advantages of a coastal site were in Tasmania. The Derwent ironworks of 1873 to 1876 situated on Battery Point in Hobart, just south of Princes Park, with a frontage on to the Derwent, is a prototype of Port Kembla or Newcastle.[12] The Redbill Point works, with its own deep-water wharf on the Tamar estuary, did not import iron ore but it did pioneer the purchase of coking coal from another state, as it increasingly replaced its original charcoal fuel with coal from the Hunter River of New South Wales coked on Redbill Point. The siting of both Battery Point and Redbill Point on estuaries accessible to ocean-going ships had no immediate effect on the pragmatic decisions of other ironmasters, except perhaps Algernon Swift, also on the Tamar. The apparent advantages of inland Lithgow dominated New South Wales' thinking for 30 years after the closure of the Tamar works. The small blast-furnace (now completely destroyed) built in Wollongong in 1882 by the manager of Mount Pleasant Colliery, Patrick Lahiff, used coke produced by spontaneous combustion in coal dumps; both the iron ore and limestone were to be locally mined but only a trial smelting was achieved.[13] The enterprise bears little resemblance to Hoskins' Port Kembla nearby, save in the use of Illawarra coking coal.

This book has deliberately excluded the brave new world of the great coastal plants at Newcastle, Port Kembla and Whyalla. It has also excluded consideration of the iron ore deposits in Western Australia, the Northern Territory and Queensland. In 1918 Queensland did have one attempt at smelting the ore from Mount Biggenden in 'a rudimentary cold-blast-furnace' at the Ipswich railway workshops; but the single test smelt of 17 April 1918 'produced the only iron ever smelted in Queensland'.[14]

The amounts of iron successfully produced from local ores in Tasmania, Victoria and South Australia were tiny, and the future in the twentieth century lay in New South Wales. The iron industry had been pioneered at Mittagong where it lasted far longer in intermittent production than in any other colonial works, and the critical importance of Lithgow in creating an almost-modern smelting plant cannot be overstated. Despite the competition of the fully modern ironworks at Newcastle, Lithgow still survived for more than another decade, and its equipment made a tangible link with the future at Port Kembla after 1928. The creation of the two huge deep-water works made it possible for other states—South Australia, Western Australia and Tasmania (at Savage River)—to participate as suppliers of iron ore to an industry which had come home to its parent state. All this stemmed from a renewal of confidence in the 1890s. Joseph Mitchell, an Illawarra coal-magnate, had summed up this renewal of confidence in Australian iron in a lecture in 1895: 'It has been well said that iron and coal combined are the sinews of industry and the master key of trade and the nation is wisest that uses most of them. Iron in its manufacture alone employs more labour than any other industry ... It is the backbone of progress and the mainstay of all true civilisation.'[15]

The ruins of Lal Lal, Bogalong, Ilfracombe and Lithgow furnaces are more than spectacular archaeological sites: they are surviving testimony to human investment, to management and workers who, in a spirit of imaginative creativity, laced with invincible optimism, first adapted the experience of an older European world to give Australian 'progress' a 'backbone' and its civilization a mainstay in the final Age of Iron.

ENDNOTES

Introduction: The Age of Iron

1   D. Diderot, 'Forges', in *Encyclopédie, ou Dictionnaire Raisonné des Sciences, des Arts, et des Métiers*, Paris 1758, VII, 153.

2   N. Elias, *The Civilising Process: The History of Manners*, 1939, translated E. Jephcott, New York 1978, I, 70–1.

3   A. Ure, *A Dictionary of Arts, Manufactures and Mines: Containing a Clear Exposition of their Principles and Practice*, 4th edn (2 vols), London 1853, I, 1060.

4   J. B. Austin, 'Mines and Minerals of South Australia' in W. Harcus (ed.), *South Australia and its History, Resources, and Productions*, London 1876, 306.

5   J. D. Muhly, 'The Beginnings of Metallurgy in the Old World' in R. Maddin (ed.), *The Beginning of the Use of Metals and Alloys*, Cambridge, Mass. 1988, 2.

6   S. Hunt, *Journal of Iron and Steel Institute*, 3, 1871, 103, quoted in *Encyclopaedia Britannica*, 9th edn, Edinburgh 1880, XIII, 336.

7   D. H. Avery, N. J. van der Merwe and S. Saitowitz, 'The Metallurgy of the Iron Bloomery in Africa', in Maddin, (ed.), *Beginning of Use of Metals and Alloys*, Cambridge, Mass. 1988, 261.

8   C. R. Alder Wright, 'Iron', *Encyclopaedia Britannica*, 9th edn, Edinburgh 1880, XIII, 358–9.

9   Ibid., 358.

10   Ibid., 359.

11   C. C. Gillespie (ed.), *A Diderot Pictorial Encyclopedia of Trades and Industry*, New York 1959, I, before plate 82.

12   S. D. Smith, C. P. Stripling and J. M. Brannon, *A Cultural Resource Survey of Tennessee's Western Highland Rim Iron Industry, 1790s–1930s*, Tennessee Department of Conservation, Division of Archaeology, Research Series 8, Nashville 1988, 46–51.

13   *Hopewell Furnace: A Guide to Hopewell Village National Historic Site, Pennsylvania*, National Park Handbook 124, Washington 1983, 24–67.

14   *Dictionary of National Biography*, *sub* J. B. Neilson.

15   Smith, Stripling and Brannon, 50, 105–6.

16   D. Morgan Rees, *Mines, Mills and Furnaces: An Introduction to Industrial Archaeology in Wales*, London 1969, 52–61; D. Morgan Rees, *The Industrial Archaeology of Wales*, Newton Abbot 1975, 29–45.

17   Rees, *Mines*, 81; Rees, *Industrial Archaeology*, 58–60.

18   Ure, I, 1070.

19   *The Dictionary of Welsh Biography Down to 1940*, London 1959, *sub* Hill family, 357; Rees, *Mines*, 70–1.

20   Rees, *Mines*, 66; A. H. John and Glanmor Williams (eds), *Glamorgan County History*, V, *Industrial Glamorgan from 1700 to 1900*, Cardiff 1980, 106.

21   Rees, *Mines*, 55–8; John and Williams, 108–16.

22 J. Lloyd, *The Early History of the Old South Wales Iron Works*, London 1906, 87.

1   First Blast: The Fitzroy Ironworks at Mittagong, New South Wales

1   Mitchell Library, Norton Smith Papers, Gibbes' Trust, A5317–2, no. 111, 167–9.
2   R. Else-Mitchell, *Early Industries in the Mittagong District*, Berrima District Historical Society 1981 (reprinted from *Journal of Royal Australian Historical Society* 26, 1940, 418–78), 4.
3   Ibid.
4   *Catalogue of the Natural and Industrial Products of New South Wales Exhibited in the Australian Museum by the Paris Exhibition Commissioners, Sydney, November 1854*, Sydney 1854, 58.
5   Else-Mitchell, 4–7.
6   *Catalogue of the Natural and Industrial Products,* 59.
7   J. L. N. Southern and J. E. A. Platt, *The History of Ironmaking in Australia, 1848–1914*, Port Kembla 1986, 23; N. R. Wills, *Economic Development of the Australian Iron and Steel Industry*, Sydney 1948, 18; Else-Mitchell, 62.
8   Else-Mitchell, 10–17.
9   Minute-book of Fitzroy Ironworks Company 1864–72 (unpublished; 16 August 1864), 4.
10 *Australian Dictionary of Biography*, 6, 333–4.
11 Fitzroy Minute-book (14 October 1864), 43.
12 Ibid. (9 September 1864), 25–8.
13 Ibid., 49, 57, 79.
14 Ibid., 89.
15 Ibid., 105–6; *Sydney Morning Herald*, 5 May 1865.
16 Fitzroy Minute-book (2 June 1865), 114.
17 Ibid., 144.
18 Ibid. (7 December 1865), 172.
19 Ure, 4th edn, I, 1070–7 and figures 794 to 800. It must be this edition since the Fitzroy set was in two volumes: the 5th edition of Ure in 1860 was expanded to three volumes.
20 Fitzroy Minute-book (30 January 1866), 190–1.
21 Company brochure, no date, pasted into Fitzroy Minute-book (11 January 1866), 184. John and George Russell were brothers of Peter Nicol Russell and partners in P. N. Russell & Co. (P. H. Russell, 'Sir Peter Nicol Russell, 1816–1905: His Family and Associates, Pioneers of the Australian Iron and Engineering Industry', *Journal of Royal Australian Historical Society*, 50, 1964, 131, 134–6.)
22 Fitzroy Minute-book (1 March 1866), 202–3.
23 Ibid. (26 April 1866), 212; (3 May 1866), 214.
24 *Sydney Morning Herald*, 31 May 1867.
25 Else-Mitchell, 23–4.
26 Fitzroy Minute-book, Levick's report (30 January 1868), 280–90.
27 Ibid., 288.
28 Ibid.
29 Ibid., 289.
30 Ibid. (1 May and report of 30 July 1868), 304, 316.

31 H. Hughes, *The Australian Iron and Steel Industry, 1848–1962*, Parkville 1964, 9.

32 Fitzroy Minute-book, Levick's report of 2 January 1869, 333.

33 E. Higginbotham and R. I. Jack, 'The Asgard Swamp Mine and Kiln Near Mt Victoria NSW', *Australian Archaeology*, 15, 1982, 54–66.

34 Fitzroy Minute-book (30 July 1869), 347.

35 Else-Mitchell, 24–5.

36 Fitzroy Minute-book (28 October 1872), 376–9.

37 Articles of Association of Mittagong Land Co. Ltd, AONSW 3/5681/556.

38 Fitzroy Minute-book (26 August 1864), 16.

39 Mitchell Library, Sub-division plans NSW, Mittagong; partly reproduced in T. Mooney, *Southern Highlands Discovery*, Bowral 1991.

40 J. B. Jaquet, *Iron Ore Deposits of New South Wales*, Geology 2, Sydney 1901, map in folder; *Town and Country Journal*, 25 March 1876.

41 Else-Mitchell, 26.

42 Ibid., 31–2.

2   Smelting Beside the Tamar

1 D. F. Branagan, *Geology and Coal Mining in the Hunter Valley, 1791–1861*, Newcastle History Monograph 6, Newcastle 1972, 11–22.

2 *Historical Records of New South Wales*, 4, 732, quoted in Branagan, 24.

3 M. Morris-Nunn and C. B. Tassell, *Tamar Valley Industrial Heritage: A Survey*, Launceston 1984, 17; W. H. Twelvetrees and A. McI. Reid, *The Iron Ore Deposits of Tasmania*, Tasmania Department of Mines, Geological Survey, Mineral Resources, 6, 1919, 4; Queen Victoria Museum and Art Gallery, *Launceston: A Pictorial History*, Launceston 1989, 3–5.

4 *Historical Records of Australia*, 3rd series 1, 664, 770, cited in Morris-Nunn and Tassell, 17.

5 Morris-Nunn and Tassell, 17.

6 G. W. Evans, *A Geographical, Historical, and Topographical Description of Van Diemen's Land*, London 1822, 58.

7 Ibid.

8 W. Mann, *Six Years' Residence in the Australian Colonies Ending in 1839*, London 1839, cited in Morris-Nunn and Tassell, 18.

9 The photograph was taken by Henry Button (Queen Victoria Museum, Launceston 1986, PO803). Coultman Smith said brusquely that the date of 1860 is 'obviously wrong' (*Town with a History: Beaconsfield Tasmania*, rev. edn, Beaconsfield 1985, 20).

10 P. S. Staughton and R.W. P. Ashley, 'The Lal Lal Blast Furnace Reserve Report'(unpublished), n.p., 1976, 123.

11 Morris-Nunn and Tassell, 3–5.

12 D. Cash, 'A Dream Unfulfilled: The Rise and Fall of Iron Smelting in Tasmania, 1872–1878', unpublished paper delivered and distributed at ANZAAS Conference 1982, 2–6.

13 G. Davison, *The Rise and Fall of Marvellous Melbourne*, Melbourne 1978, 6.

14 There has been some doubt about the location of Harrison's furnace. Coultman Smith believed that it was at Redbill Point (*Beaconsfield*, 25). There is conclusive evidence, however, that it was not at Redbill Point. Harrison himself wrote in a reminiscent letter in 1902 that 'I accordingly put up a furnace

on the mines' (Twelvetrees and Reid, 5). The local newspaper confirms this: 'close to the township on Anderson's Creek [Leonardsburgh] the company have erected the first furnace' (*Cornwall Courier*, 18 April 1873).

15 Morris-Nunn and Tassell, 25, quoting *Cornwall Chronicle*, 4 November 1872. This is a month before the foundation stone of the blast-furnace was laid.

16 *Launceston Examiner*, 17 May 1873, 2.

17 *Illustrated Australian News*, 29 December 1875, 204; 10 July 1876, 105; *Illustrated Sydney News*, 12 November 1875, 8; 22 July 1876, 9; *Australasian Sketcher*, 8 July 1876, 52. The *Illustrated Sydney News*, 27 September 1873, 9, after the failure of Harrison's furnace but before the next stage, portrayed the original short jetty, the iron-mines on Mount Vulcan and the tramway (these 1873 lithographs were from photographs by H. A. Bayley of Hobart).

18 Morris-Nunn and Tassell, 23–38; Southern and Platt, *The History of Ironmaking in Australia 1848–1914*, Port Kembla 1986, 39–45 (based on Morris-Nunn and Tassell); Cash, ANZAAS paper; T. C. Just in R. M. Johnston, *Tasmanian Official Record 1891*, Hobart 1892, 460–70.

19 Morris-Nunn and Tassell, 38, citing *Cornwall Chronicle*, 3 August 1877.

20 Twelvetrees and Reid, 8; Morris-Nunn and Tassell, 38 (both citing T. C. Just in Johnston, *Tasmanian Official Record 1891*, 470).

21 *Illustrated Australian News*, 10 July 1876, 105, repeated in *Illustrated Sydney News*, 22 July 1876, 9; reproduced in C. Craig, *Old Tasmanian Prints*, Launceston 1964, 244.

22 Twelvetrees and Reid, 17.

23 Australian Academy of Technological Sciences and Engineering, *Technology in Australia, 1788–1988*, Melbourne 1988, 639–40.

24 Cash, ANZAAS paper, 7.

25 *Launceston Examiner*, 20 September 1873, 5 quoting assay of 15 September 1872.

26 Ibid.

27 *Border Post* (Albury), 4 April 1874, 3, reprinted in *Yass Courier*, 7 April 1874, which is the source of the transcript in Southern and Platt, 29–30.

28 *Cornwall Chronicle*, 8 August, 5 September 1873.

29 *Launceston Examiner*, 29 November 1873; *Cornwall Chronicle*, 29 December 1873.

30 *Cornwall Chronicle*, 29 December 1873.

31 Ibid.

32 *Cornwall Chronicle*, 9 December 1874.

33 Ibid.

34 *Cornwall Chronicle*, 23 February 1874.

35 *Launceston Examiner*, 20 September 1873, 5.

36 *Dictionary of National Biography*, *sub* James, Baird.

37 *Launceston Examiner*, 20 September 1873, 5.

38 Ibid.

39 See the 1932 photographs of charcoal-burning heaps at Cookamidgera, beyond Parkes (A. Davies, *At Work and Play: Our Past in Pictures*, Sydney 1989, 102).

40 F. Overman, *The Manufacture of Iron in all its Various Branches*, 3rd edn, Philadelphia 1854, 110–12.

41 *Launceston Examiner*, 20 September 1873, 5.

42 *Border Post* (Albury), 8 April 1874, 3; *Yass Courier*, 26 May 1874, 2.

43 *Launceston Examiner*, 20 September 1873, 5.

44 Information supplied by Mr Craig Sheehan, the owner of Ilfracombe, 1992.

45 H. Wellington, *The Ilfracombe Blast Furnace 1872: An Historical and Technical Study of One of Australia's Earliest Iron Smelters*, Grubb Shaft Museum, Beaconsfield 1992; D. K. Reynolds, 'The Ilfracombe Iron Company, Beaconsfield, Tasmania: A Report of Site Inspections and the Interpretations of the Observations of the Evidence Found from those Inspections Made during February and March 1992', unpublished, June 1992. I am grateful to both Mr Wellington and Mr Reynolds for their willingness to discuss their findings with me.

46 *Launceston Examiner*, 20 September 1873, 5.

47 *Cornwall Chronicle*, 9 December 1874.

48 Morris-Nunn and Tassell, 39.

49 *Australasian Sketcher*, 8 July 1876, 52. But this sketch was not drawn on site to judge by the artist's failure to show the jetty or the beach. Instead the artist shows a wooden fence.

50 Morris-Nunn and Tassell, 12.

51 *Launceston Examiner*, 20 September 1873, 5.

52 Ibid.

53 There was a fourth, which has left no remains at all and is therefore not discussed in this book. It was in Hobart, at Battery Point. The Derwent Iron Works operated from 1873 until 1876 with little success. It too was an old-style furnace, with a brick shaft on a square stone base. The only representation of it seems to be in a general view of Hobart from the Derwent published in the *Australasian Sketcher* on 10 May 1879, and reproduced in Clifford Craig's *Old Tasmanian Prints*, 230.

54 Wills, 16; Hughes, 12; Cash, 16.

3   From Gold to Iron in Victoria: The Lal Lal Furnace

1 W. Bate, *Lucky City: The First Generation at Ballarat, 1851–1901*, Carlton 1978, 207.

2 Ibid., 213.

3 Staughton and Ashley, 83; J. Bonwick, 'The Victorian Iron Mine', *Iron*, new series 7, no. 172, 29 April 1876, 546.

4 H. S. Elford and M. R. McKeown, *Coal Mining in Australia*, Melbourne and Sydney 1947, 200–5.

5 Bonwick, 546.

6 G. Brown, 'Coal Resources of Victoria', *Mining and Geological Journal*, 3, iv, September 1948, 11; D. E. Thomas and W. Baragwanath, 'Geology of the Brown Coals of Victoria', *Mining and Geological Journal*, 4, ii, September 1950, 52–5; 'A Visit to the Lignite Deposits at Lal Lal, near Ballaarat', *Dicker's Mining Record*, 3, June 1864, 101.

7 K. Brown, *1788–1988, Australia's Bicentenary: A Record of the Lal Lal Community's Part in the Celebrations with a Short History of the Area*, Lal Lal 1988, 45.

8 E. J. Dunn, 'Notes on Fireclay and Iron Ore Deposits at Lal Lal', unpublished report, Geological Survey of Victoria, 4 July 1910, Department of Manufacturing and Industry Development (Victoria) Library, report 1910/995,1.

9   'A Visit to the Lignite Deposits at Lal Lal', 100–1.

10 Staughton and Ashley, 84, 119.

11 Bonwick, 546.

12 F. M. Krause, 'The Lal Lal Iron Ore Deposits', *School of Mines, Ballaarat, Annual Report presented at the Meeting of Governors, held February 9th, 1881*, Ballarat 1881, 49.

13 F. M. Krause, 'Lal Lal' report, 17 August 1877, transcribed in A. M. Hewitt et al., 'General Notes on Important Iron Ore Deposits in the State of Victoria', unpublished report to Geological Survey of Victoria, 21 November 1910, Department of Manufacturing and Industry Development (Victoria) Library, report 1910/1756, 8. The original 1877 manuscript has been lost or mislaid.

14 *An Outline of the Various Enterprises on the Extensive Mineral Deposits at Lal Lal, Victoria, Dating from 1857, and Incorporating the Developmental Work of Pulverized Coal Australasia Limited in Association with the Victorian Central Coal & Iron Mining Coy. N.L.—1919–1943*, n.p. [c. 1978], 3. The historic information comes in part from the Capel family who ran the Lal Lal store in the 1860s. There is no other source for Rowley's experimental shaft-furnace.

15 For example, R. I. Jack, 'The Iron and Steel Industry' in J. Birmingham, I. Jack and D. Jeans, *Australian Pioneer Technology: Sites and Relics*, Richmond Vic. 1979, 93.

16 This sketch-map has been lost or mislaid along with Krause's report of 1877 but was fortunately published in R. Ashley et al., 'The Lal Lal Iron Tramway', *Light Railways*, 9, no. 34, Summer 1970–1, 25.

17 Staughton and Ashley, 84.

18 Ashley et al., 6.

19 Ibid., 6.

20 Bonwick, 546; Staughton and Ashley, 167–8.

21 Staughton and Ashley, 167–8.

22 Ibid., 168. They claim that charcoal sites are visible near the former tramway beside the present car-park.

23 *Illustrated Australian News*, no. 270, 28 November 1878, 196, 202.

24 Bate, 44, 50, 102, 128, 217, 230; Ashley et al., 7.

25 Staughton and Ashley, after p. 72 (reproduction of 1883 circular).

26 W. Baragwanath, 'Note on the Iron Smelting Furnace, Lal Lal', *Annual Report of the Secretary for Mines . . . for the Year 1910*, Melbourne 1911, 66.

27 'Blast Furnace in the Bush', *BHP Review*, 45, i, Autumn 1968, 11–12.

28 For the racecourse, see K. Brown's centenary history of Lal Lal, 43, 45.

29 Ashley et al., 6.

30 Baragwanath, 66.

31 Staughton and Ashley, after p. 177.

32 Bonwick, 546.

33 The best summation of these developments is in Southern and Platt, 62–3.

34 Bate, 212, 215.

35 Victorian Department of Lands plan L2322, reproduced in Staughton and Ashley, after p. 99.

36 Ashley et al., 9–15; Staughton and Ashley, 101–7, 147–53.

37 Ashley et al., 13.

38 Ibid.

39 Ibid., 14.

40 Ibid., 25.

41 Ibid., 16; Staughton and Ashley, inserted plan; Southern and Platt, fig. 16, p. 72. The Ashley plan printed by Southern and Platt is on display on the information board at the ironworks site and is the basis for our figure on p. 68.

42 Ashley et al., 12.

43 Ibid., 20–1; Bate, 215.

44 Bargwanath, 66.

45 Staughton and Ashley, 116.

46 Ibid., 168.

47 *Courier* (Ballarat), 6 July 1891, 2, cited in Ashley et al., 21.

48 Department of Manufacturing and Industry Development, Mineral Branch Library, P622.09945 (943), published in *Annual Report of the Secretary of Mines . . . for the Year 1910*, after p. 66; P622.09945 (944).

4   Experiment in South Australia: Mount Jagged

1   BHP, *Seventy-Five Years of BHP Development in Industry*, [1960], 15–48.

2   *Bunyip*, 9 November 1872, quoted in E. H. Coombe, *History of Gawler, 1837 to 1908*, Gawler 1910, 351 (cf. E. G. Robertson & J. Robertson, *Cast Iron Decoration: A World Survey*, London 1977, 51, where the date of Martin's inscription is given wrongly as 1876).

3   D. A. Cumming and G. Moxham, *They Built South Australia: Engineers, Technicians, Manufacturers, Contractors and their Work*, Adelaide 1986, 40–1.

4   H. Y. L. Brown, *A Record of the Mines of South Australia: Specially Prepared for the Mining Exhibition*, Adelaide 1890, 125, quoting a statement by Dubois written in 1887.

5   H. Bauerman, *A Treatise on the Metallurgy of Iron, Containing Outlines of the History of Iron Manufactures, Methods of Assay and Analyses of Iron Ores, Processes of Manufacture of Iron and Steel etc.*, 1st edn, London 1868; 3rd edn, London 1872; 4th edn, London 1874.

6   *Illustrated Adelaide News*, January 1875, quoted in full in G. R. Needham and D. I. Thomson, *Men of Metal: A Chronicle of the Metal-Casting Industry in South Australia, 1836–1986*, Adelaide 1987, 47–9.

7   H. Y. L. Brown, 125. 'Lithofracteur' was the brand name of dynamite specifically for mining use introduced by Nobel about 1867. It was superseded by gelignite after 1875 (J. Read, *Explosives*, Harmondsworth 1942, 100). I am grateful to Dr Peter Bell for this reference.

8   Fitzroy Minute-book (20 November 1865), 168–9.

9   Wright, 291.

10 *Sydney Morning Herald*, 27 July 1868, 5.

11 Fitzroy Minute-book (30 January 1868), 282.

12 *Goulburn Herald*, 2 September 1876, quoted in Else-Mitchell, 28.

13 J. Birmingham, 'Gold', in Birmingham, Jack and Jeans, 57.

14 Ivar Bohm, *The Swedish Blast Furnace in the 19th Century*, Jernkontorets Bergshistoriska Utskott, series H, no. 7, 1972, English version 1974, 31.

15 South Australian Department of Mines, *Mining Review*, 23, 1915, 40–1.

16 Austin, 306.

17 Needham and Thomson, 49.

18 Austin, 306.

5   The Forgotten Furnace: Bogolong, New South Wales

1   Southern and Platt, 29–30.
2   Jaquet, 146.
3   *Yass Courier,* 21 November 1873. We are grateful to Dr R. Ward for this reference.
4   *The English Mechanic and World of Science,* 18, no. 460, 16 January 1874, 426–7. It is mentioned and neatly condensed in the *Border Post* (Albury), 28 March 1874, 4.
5   Jaquet, 146.
6   Ibid.
7   Ibid.; *Border Post* (Albury), 8 April 1874, 3.
8   *The Australian Handbook and Almanac . . . for 1879,* Sydney 1879, 127.
9   *Border Post* (Albury), 4 April 1874, 3; *Yass Courier,* 7 April 1874, 2.
10 *Greville's Official Post Office Directory of New South Wales,* Sydney 1872, 55–6; *Greville's Official Post Office Directory and Gazetteer of New South Wales . . . 1875 to 1877,* Sydney n.d., 76.
11 *Bailliere's New South Wales Gazetteer and Road Guide,* Sydney 1866, 621.
12 *Greville's Directory, 1875–7,* 56. The brick-maker was not listed in Greville's 1872 *Directory,* 41–2.
13 *Border Post* (Albury), 8 April 1874, 3.
14 Ibid. Although the *Border Post* claims to be republishing these details from the *Yass Courier,* the information did not appear in that newspaper.
15 *Border Post* (Albury), 4 April 1874, 3; *Yass Courier,* 7 April 1874, 2.
16 *Border Post* (Albury), 30 May 1874, 3.
17 Ibid.; *Yass Courier,* 26 May 1874, 2.
18 *Greville's Directory, 1872,* 55–6; *Greville's Directory, 1875–7,* 75–6.
19 Cf. the 1874 map of County Harden in the Mitchell Library.
20 A. Andrews, *The History of Albury, 1824–1895,* Albury 1912, reprinted 1988, 62–75; *The Border Post (Albury) Almanac for 1878,* reprinted North Sydney 1979, advertisements.

6   Creating a Steel Town: Lithgow, New South Wales

1   The source material for the Zig-Zag is most conveniently presented by W. A. Bayley, *The Great Zig-Zag Railway at Lithgow,* Bulli 1977.
2   For the industrial development of the area, the best secondary works are two unpublished undergraduate theses in Economic History: R.W. Downey, 'Lithgow as an Industrial Centre: History of Industry in Lithgow, 1870–1912', University of Sydney, BA Hons thesis, 1972 and R. J. McInnes, 'Lithgow, 1869–1930: An Outline Economic History of the Town', University of NSW, B. Comm. thesis, 1972. For existing sites associated with coal, coke, iron, copper and brewing, see Birmingham, Jack and Jeans, 76, 93–8, 110–18, 172–3. For an overview, see A. Cremin, 'The Growth of an Industrial Valley: Lithgow, New South Wales', *Australian Journal of Historical Archaeology,* 7, 1989, 35–42.
3   E. J. McKenzie, *Thomas Brown, Founder of Lithgow and his Home, Esk Bank,* Katoomba 1969, 3.
4   R. I. Jack, 'Historical Introduction' in A. C. Cremin (ed.), *Survey of Sites of Historical Interest in the Lithgow Area 1981,* Sydney 1987, chapter 1.

5   Hughes, 18–19; Wills, 26–8; Southern and Platt, 28.

6   Wills, 29.

7   Hughes, 20.

8   Quoted in Wills, 28.

9   Southern and Platt, 28–9; *National Advocate*, 16 January 1894.

10 G. Blainey, *The Steel Master: A Life of Essington Lewis*, Melbourne 1971, 199.

11 J. J. Alexander and W. R. Hooper, *The History of Great Torrington in the County of Devon*, Sutton 1948, 177.

12 W. White, *History, Gazetteer and Directory of Devonshire*, Sheffield 1850, 752; M. Billing, *M. Billing's Directory and Gazetteer of the County of Devon*, Birmingham 1857, 301; J. G. Harrod, *J.G. Harrod's Royal County Directory of Devonshire and Cornwall*, Norwich 1878, 708; W. White, *History, Gazetteer and Directory of Devonshire*, Sheffield 1878–9, 461.

13 Hughes, 26.

14 Alexander and Harper, 177.

15 J. Lysaght (Aust.) Pty. Ltd., *Lysaght Venture*, Sydney 1955, 1–3.

16 J. A. Perkins, 'William Sandford', *Australian Dictionary of Biography*, 11, 521.

17 Sandford Papers, Mitchell Library, MSS 1556, box 1, item 5, p. 26 (ML MSS 1556/1/5, 26).

18 Sandford Papers, ML MSS 1556/1/5, 51.

19 W. F. Morrison, *The Aldine Centennial History of New South Wales*, Sydney 1888, II, Lithgow biographies; *Bathurst Daily Times*, 15 August 1882, 21 January 1884, 2 November 1886.

20 Rutherford's reminiscences, *National Advocate*, 2 December 1911; A. [Cremin] Madden, 'The Esk Bank Iron Works Lease, 1887', *Australian Society for Historical Archaeology Newsletter*, 10, i, March 1980, 25–7.

21 *Bathurst Daily Times*, 23 March 1891.

22 Sandford Papers, ML MSS 1556/2/4,5, 1g–34.

23 *National Advocate*, 2 December 1911.

24 Sandford Papers, ML MSS 1556/1/2, fol. 40v.

25 Ibid., 1556/1/3, fol. 19d.

26 Ibid., fol. 1d.

27 Ibid., fol. 18v.

28 Ibid., 1556/1/5, 29.

29 Wills, 32; Southern and Platt, 91.

30 Sir Cecil Hoskins, *The Hoskins Saga*, Sydney 1969, 36; *Sydney Mail*, 1 April 1903.

31 Sandford Papers, ML MSS 1556/1/2, fol. 40v.

32 Ibid., 1556/1/3, fol. 4v.

33 *Lithgow Mercury*, 4 August 1899.

34 Wills, 48.

35 Sandford Papers, ML MSS 1556/1/4, 3.

36 Ibid., 1556/1/5, 4.

37 Ibid., 13.

38 Ibid., 1556/1/4, 53.

39 Ibid., 1556/1/1, fol. 25d.

40 Ibid., 1556/1/4, 29.

41 Ibid., 1556/1/6, 2.

42 Alexander and Hooper, 178.

43 Port Kembla, Lithgow engineering drawings nos. 1198, 1253, 1254, 1255, 1260, 1261; Sandford Papers, ML MSS 1556/1/4, 68–9.
44 Ibid., 1556/1/7, 43.
45 Wills, 48.
46 Sandford Papers, ML MSS 1556/2/14; 1556/1/7, 95.
47 Ibid., 1556/1/5, 73–5; 1556/1/7, 39.
48 Wills, 48.
49 Cf. ibid., 50.
50 Sandford Papers, ML MSS 1556/1/4, 9–10.
51 Ibid., 1556/2/40, 197.
52 *Lithgow Mercury*, 24 April 1906.
53 Sandford Papers, ML MSS 1556/1/4, 9.
54 A. Linters, *Industria: Industrial Architecture in Belgium*, Liège and Brussels 1986, 28–30.

7 *The Lithgow Blast-furnaces*

1 R. F. Wylie and C. C. Singleton, 'The Railway Crossing of the Blue Mountains, 7, Lithgow', *Australian Railway Historical Society Bulletin*, new series 10, no. 257, March 1959, 37, 41.
2 Sandford Papers, ML MSS 1556/1/4, 68–9.
3 Ibid., 73.
4 Sandford Papers, ML MSS 1556/1/7, 103.
5 *Lithgow Mercury*, 23 March, 3 April, 1 June 1906; Sandford Papers, ML MSS 1556/4x, 217.
6 *Lithgow Mercury*, 24 April 1906.
7 J. E. Carne, *Geology and Mineral Resources of the Western Coalfield*, Memoirs of Geological Survey of NSW, Geology 6, Sydney 1908, 230–1; *Lithgow Mercury*, 20, 24, 27 July; 10, 31 August 1906.
8 *Lithgow Mercury*, 1 June 1906.
9 Wylie and Singleton, 41.
10 Sandford Papers, ML MSS 1556/1/4, 102; *Lithgow Mercury*, 30 November 1906.
11 NSW Department of Mines, *Annual Report*, 1906, 33; 1907, 36, 98.
12 Sandford Papers, ML MSS 1556/1/4, 68–9.
13 Ibid., 1556/2/12.
14 Ibid., 1556/1/4, 9.
15 NSW Dept of Mines, *Annual Report*, 1907, 60.
16 *Lithgow Mercury*, 30 April; 3, 13, 15 May 1907; *Sydney Morning Herald*, 1 May 1907; Sandford Papers, ML MSS 1556/4x, 233–5.
17 Borchard's report of 12 November 1907 in *NSW Legislative Assembly: Votes and Proceedings*, 1907, 2nd Session, 'Development of Iron and Steel Industry', 12–13.
18 Ibid., 14–17.
19 Wills, 55.
20 Ibid., 55–6.
21 *Lithgow Mercury*, 9 December 1907.
22 *Lithgow Mercury*, 11 December 1907.
23 Sandford Papers, ML MSS 1556/3/1/7; *Lithgow Mercury*, 4 August 1899.
24 Sandford Papers, ML MSS 1556/1/4, 87.

25 *Votes and Proceedings Legislative Assembly of NSW*, 1907, 18.

26 Sandford Papers, ML MSS 1556/1/7, 66.

27 The speech is given in full in G. & C. Hoskins Ltd., *The Iron Industry and its Development*, ('The Blue Book'), Sydney 1915, 28.

28 Sandford Papers, ML MSS 1556/1/7, 66.

29 Ibid., 71–3.

30 Wills, 57–8.

31 Sandford Papers, ML MSS 1556/1/1, fol. [10r]; ibid., 1556/1/4 *passim*.

32 Wills, 57–8.

33 R. Murray and K. White, *The Ironworkers: A History of the Federated Ironworkers' Association of Australia*, Sydney 1982, 38.

34 Hoskins, *Hoskins Saga*, 76.

35 NSW Dept of Mines, *Annual Report*, 1910, 53; 1911, 60.

36 Wills, 64–6; *Legislative Assembly of NSW: Parliamentary Papers*, 1911, 2nd Session, 'Report of Royal Commission on the Iron and Steel Industry', Hoskins' evidence, 84–99.

37 Hughes, 62.

38 Wills, 67–9.

39 *Should Lithgow Be the State Workshop?*, Lithgow 1914.

40 Hughes, 62.

41 L. F. Harper and H. P. White, *Coke*, NSW Department of Mines, Geological Survey, Bulletin 12, Sydney 1924, 36–7.

42 *Lithgow Mercury*, 2 September 1910; 7 October 1912; 20 June 1913.

43 Hoskins Papers, ML MSS 4361/1/letter book, 64.

44 Ibid., 90–7, 107.

45 Ibid., 189–90.

46 Ibid., 305, 315.

47 Ibid., 342–5.

48 Ibid., 292; *Lithgow Mercury*, 3 October 1913.

49 Hughes, 49–50.

50 Wills, 74.

51 Hughes, 63.

52 Cremin (ed.), chapter 2, 6F.

53 Wills, 79–81.

54 Hoskins Papers, ML MSS 4361/7/minute–book, 167, 191–2, 265–6.

55 Ibid., 191–2.

56 *Hoskins Iron & Steel Co.*, 'The Black Book', Sydney 1925, 29; M. Eddy, *Marulan, A Unique Heritage*, Marulan 1985, 87–8.

57 Hoskins Papers, ML MSS 4361/7/minute-book, 265–6; Harper and White, 9; Hoskins, *Hoskins Saga*, 99.

58 Hoskins Papers, ML MSS 4361/7/minute-book, 265–6.

59 Wills, 84.

60 Hoskins, *Hoskins Saga*, 103–12; *Australian Dictionary of Biography*, 9, 371–3.

61 Hoskins Papers, ML MSS 4361/7/minute-book, 311, 323.

62 A. C. Clarke, *Lithgow's Last Years as a Steel Town*, Lithgow District Historical Society, Occasional Paper 15, 1973, 3.

63 Hoskins Papers, ML MSS 4361/7/minute-book, 303–4.

64 Clarke, 6.

65 Sandford Papers, ML MSS 1556/1/4, 24, 26, 45, 106.

66 Ibid., 1556/1/7, 77, 79.
67 Ibid., 81.
68 Ibid., 71–3.
69 Ibid., 1556/2/50, 249.
70 Ibid, 1556/1/7, 66.
71 Ibid, 1556/2/50, 249.

8   Lithgow Today

1   Murray and White, 35–60.
2   For example, the Hoskins 'Black Book', 23, 25.
3   W. Astley, *The Federal Capital: An Argument for the Western Sites*, Bathurst 1903;
      T. A. Machattie, *The Federal Capital: The Case for the West*, Bathurst 1904.
4   Hoskins, *The Hoskins Saga*, 52.
5   The Hoskins 'Black Book', 42.
6   Hoskins Papers, ML MSS 4361/7/minute-book, 296, 335.
7   *Lithgow Mercury*, 12 April 1911, 16 June 1911, 21 June 1913.
8   Hoskins, *Hoskins Saga*, 112.

Conclusion

1   C. A. Jeffries, 'The Eskbank Iron Works', *The Lone Hand*, 1 June 1911, 183.
2   Essington Lewis, *Iron and Steel Industry in Australia*, n.p. 1929, 8.
3   *Illustrated Australian News*, no. 232, 29 December 1875, 210.
4   Cf. Cash, 'A Dream Unfulfilled', ANZAAS 1982, 17.
5   *Illustrated Adelaide News*, January 1875, quoted in Needham and Thomson, 49.
6   *Border Post* (Albury) 4, 8 April, 30 May 1874; *Yass Courier* 7 April, 26 May 1874.
      The *Yass Courier* notice of 7 April, which is a reprint of the *Border Post*
      article published on 4 April, is transcribed in Southern and Platt, 29–30.
7   *Illustrated Sydney News*, 27 September 1873, 6.
8   *Sydney Morning Herald*, 6, 10, 13, 14, 21 March 1865; 27, 30 July, 4, 7, 12, 17,
      21, 26, 28 August, 1 September 1868.
9   *Illustrated Sydney News*, 27 September 1873, 6. The location of the proposed
      blast-furnace site is on map 1:25000, *Lithgow 8931-III-5*, 224027; of the
      iron deposit, on map 1:25000, *Meadow Flat 8831-II-S*, 763983.
10 Cf. *Encyclopaedia Britannica,* 9th edn 1880, XIII, 359. Nine out of 44 new blast-
      furnaces in process of erection in America in 1880 were expected to use
      charcoal.
11 Cf. James Bonwick's discussion of charcoal-burners in *Iron*, 29 April 1876, 546.
12 For the location of the Derwent Iron Works see the excellent view of Hobart
      published in *Australasian Sketcher*, 10 May 1879, and republished in Craig,
      230.
13 Southern and Platt, 30–4.
14 R. L. Whitmore, *Coke Oven Technology in the Ipswich Area*, Department of
      Mining and Metallurgical Engineering, University of Queensland, 1983, 11.
15 Lecture of Joseph Mitchell, reported in *Evening News*, 30 March 1895, ML
      DOC 1089a. For Mitchell, see *Australian Dictionary of Biography*, 5, 261–2.

GLOSSARY

blast-main: the large pipe which carries the air blast to the furnace.

blast-furnace: a furnace which receives a high-pressure current or blast of hot or cold air, generated by a blower or blowing-engine. A working furnace is 'in blast'.

bloom: smelted iron which has been worked ('wrought') by hammering.

blowing in/out: commissioning/decommissioning a blast-furnace by heating or cooling it gradually.

bosh: widest part of the furnace, between the hearth and the upper container (see illustration on p. 10, B–C).

calcining: preliminary roasting or burning of iron ore to concentrate it (see illustration on p. 20).

charcoal: wood which has been charred by very slow burning to leave only carbon.

chequer bricks: refractory bricks piled up in honeycomb shape, to allow air or gases to pass through them.

coke: coal which has been reduced to carbon by heating at high temperature in a coke oven.

cupola: a chimney-like furnace for melting pig or scrap-iron, which sits on top of a coke fire.

fire-clay, fire-stone: natural clays or stone which have a fusing point of over 1600 degrees C and can therefore withstand high temperatures. The clay is used to make refractory bricks (fire-bricks).

flume: an open trough used as a channel to carry water, often made of wood.

flux: limestone or other material which both facilitates combustion and removes the impurities from iron ore; the main component of slag.

forge: to forge is to make pig-iron into wrought-iron, by hammering; the forge is the building in which this is done; the Catalan forge was a means of smelting the iron by introducing a blast of air, which was not blown but drawn down through a waterpipe (see illustration on p. 4).

foundry: the place in which iron castings are made.

furnace: a container in which iron ore or iron can be heated to melting point.

hearth: bottom part of the furnace with maximum heat (see illustration on p. 10, A).

hematite: a common form of iron oxide, named after the Greek word for blood, as it is often red in colour.

ladle: a large scoop-shaped container, lined with refractory material, for carrying melted iron.

pig-iron: iron smelted from ore. A nickname derived from the resemblance of the channels, into which smelted iron ran from the furnace, to a sow and its feeding piglets.

race: narrow channel which forces water onto a water-wheel to move it. The tail-race is the channel through which the water runs away from the wheel after having moved it.

rolling-mills: machines for shaping hot or cold iron.

reverberatory furnace: furnace in which the fuel is separate and only its heat is directed onto the metal.

refractory bricks: bricks made of fire-clay, used for example for lining blast-furnaces or ladles (see illustration on p. 10).

skull: iron which has been spoilt, for example iron which has cooled too fast, or has been mixed with slag (see illustrations on pp. 86 and 132).

slag: melted waste material, for example the flux and impurities from smelted iron ore.

smelt: to reduce iron ore to molten metal, usually by heating; a smelt is the product of this operation.

steel: a malleable alloy of iron and carbon.

tap hole: hole at the base of the blast-furnace through which the molten iron flowed. The furnace was tapped, when the iron ore had melted, by opening the tap hole, which was usually plugged by a refractory material. This plug was shot into position from a tap hole gun, powered in the nineteenth to early twentieth century by steam (see illustration on p. 110).

tuyere: Pronounced and occasionally spelt 'tweer', from the French word for pipe. Connecting pipe between the end of the blast-main and the furnace's hearth, which brings the hot or cold blast into the hearth (see illustration on p. 10, T).

BIBLIOGRAPHY

Printed Works

Alexander, J. J. and Hooper, W. R., *The History of Great Torrington in the County of Devon*, Sutton 1948.

An Outline of the Various Enterprises on the Extensive Mineral Deposits at Lal Lal, Victoria, Dating from 1857, and Incorporating the Developmental Work of Pulverized Coal Australasia Limited in Association with the Victorian Central Coal & Iron Mining Coy. N.L.—1919–1943, n.p. [*c.* 1978].

Andrews, A., *The History of Albury, 1824–1895*, Albury 1912, reprinted 1988.

Ashley, R. et al., 'The Lal Lal Iron Tramway', *Light Railways*, 9, no. 34, Summer 1970–1, 2–25.

Astley, W., *The Federal Capital: An Argument for the Western Sites*, Bathurst 1903.

Austin, J. B., 'Mines and Minerals of South Australia', in Harcus, W. (ed.), *South Australia and its History, Resources, and Productions*, London 1876, 279–312.

Australian Academy of Technological Sciences and Engineering, *Technology in Australia, 1788–1988*, Melbourne 1988.

Australian Dictionary of Biography (12 vols), Melbourne 1963–90.

The Australian Handbook and Almanac . . . for 1879, Sydney 1879.

Avery, D. H., van der Merwe, N. J. and Saitowitz, S., 'The Metallurgy of the Iron Bloomery in Africa', in Maddin, R. (ed.), *The Beginning of the Use of Metals and Alloys*, Cambridge Mass. 1988, 261–82.

Bailliere's New South Wales Gazetteer and Road Guide, Sydney 1866.

Baragwanath, W., 'Note on the Iron Smelting Furnace, Lal Lal', *Annual Report of the Secretary for Mines . . . for the Year 1910*, Melbourne 1911, 66.

Bate, W., *Lucky City: The First Generation at Ballarat, 1851–1901*, Carlton 1978.

Bauerman, H., *A Treatise on the Metallurgy of Iron, Containing Outlines of the History of Iron Manufactures, Methods of Assay and Analyses of Iron Ores, Processes of Manufacture of Iron and Steel etc.*, 1st edn, London 1868; 3rd edn, London 1872; 4th edn, London 1874.

Bayley, W. A., *The Great Zig-Zag Railway at Lithgow*, Bulli 1977.

BHP, *Seventy-Five Years of BHP Development in Industry*, [1960], 15–48.

Billing, M., *M. Billing's Directory and Gazetteer of the County of Devon*, Birmingham 1857.

Birmingham, J., 'Gold', in Birmingham, J., Jack, I. and Jeans, D., *Australian Pioneer Technology: Sites and Relics*, Richmond Vic. 1979, 35–58.

Birmingham, J., Jack, I. and Jeans, D., *Australian Pioneer Technology: Sites and Relics*, Richmond Vic. 1979.

'A Bit of a Change After Sydney' [Iron Knob, SA], *BHP Review*, 44, iv, Winter 1967, 5–8.

Blainey, G., *The Steel Master: A Life of Essington Lewis*, Melbourne 1971.

BIBLIOGRAPHY

'Blast Furnace in the Bush', *BHP Review*, 45, i, Autumn 1968, 8–12.

Bohm, I., *The Swedish Blast Furnace in the 19th Century*, Jernkontorets Bergshistoriska Utskott, series H, no. 7, 1972, English version 1974.

Bonwick, J., 'The Victorian Iron Mine', *Iron*, new series 7, no. 172, 29 April 1876, 546.

Border Post Almanac for 1878 (Albury), reprinted North Sydney 1979.

Branagan, D. F., *Geology and Coal Mining in the Hunter Valley, 1791–1861*, Newcastle History Monograph 6, Newcastle 1972.

Brown, G., 'Coal Resources of Victoria', *Mining and Geological Journal*, 3, iv, September 1948, 4–15.

Brown, H. Y. L., *A Record of the Mines of South Australia: Specially Prepared for the Mining Exhibition*, Adelaide 1890.

Brown, K., *1788–1988, Australia's Bicentenary: A Record of the Lal Lal Community's Part in the Celebrations with a Short History of the Area*, Lal Lal 1988.

Carne, J. E., *Geology and Mineral Resources of the Western Coalfield*, Memoirs of Geological Survey of NSW, Geology 6, Sydney 1908.

Carroll, B., 'Ballarat Lace', *Walkabout*, 35, ix, September 1969, 34–5.

Catalogue of the Natural and Industrial Products of New South Wales Exhibited in the Australian Museum by the Paris Exhibition Commissioners, Sydney, November 1854, Sydney 1854.

Clarke, A. C., *Lithgow's Last Years as a Steel Town*, Lithgow District Historical Society, Occasional Paper 15, 1973.

Coombe, E. H., *History of Gawler, 1837 to 1908*, Gawler 1910, 351.

Craig, C., *Old Tasmanian Prints*, Launceston 1964.

Cremin, A., 'The Blast Furnace at Lithgow, NSW, and the Presentation of Ironmaking Sites', *Fourth National Conference on Engineering Heritage 1988*, The Institution of Engineers Australia, 1988, 52–8.

Cremin, A., 'The Growth of an Industrial Valley: Lithgow, New South Wales', *Australian Journal of Historical Archaeology*, 7, 1989, 35–42.

Cremin, A. C. (ed.), *Survey of Sites of Historical Interest in the Lithgow Area 1981*, Sydney 1987.

Cremin, A. and Jack, I., 'Australia's First Modern Blast Furnace: Lithgow, New South Wales', *TICCIH Industrial Heritage Austria 1987, Transactions*, 2, Vienna 1990, 56–61.

[Cremin] Madden, A., 'The Esk Bank Iron Works Lease, 1887', *Australian Society for Historical Archaeology Newsletter*, 10, i, March 1980, 25–8.

Cumming, D. A. and Moxham, G., *They Built South Australia: Engineers, Technicians, Manufacturers, Contractors and their Work*, Adelaide 1986.

Dauncey, W. C., 'The Iron Deposits of Tasmania', *Papers and Proceedings of Royal Society of Tasmania for 1897*, Hobart 1898, 49–53.

Davies, A., *At Work and Play: Our Past in Pictures*, Sydney 1989.

Davison, G., *The Rise and Fall of Marvellous Melbourne*, Melbourne 1978.

Dictionary of National Biography, various editions, London.

The Dictionary of Welsh Biography Down to 1940, London 1959.

Diderot, D., *Encyclopédie, ou Dictionnaire Raisonné des Sciences, des Arts, et des Métiers* (17 vols), Paris 1751–73.

Diderot, D., *Recueil des Planches sur les Sciences, les Arts Libéraux et les Arts Méchaniques avec leur Explication* (11 vols), Paris 1762–73.

Eddy, M., *Marulan, A Unique Heritage*, Marulan 1985.

Elford, H. S. and McKeown, M. R., *Coal Mining in Australia*, Melbourne and Sydney 1947.

Elias, N., *The Civilising Process: The History of Manners* (1939), translated E. Jephcott, New York 1978.

Else-Mitchell, R., *Early Industries in the Mittagong District*, Berrima District Historical Society 1981 (reprinted from *Journal of Royal Australian Historical Society*, 26, 1940, 418–78).

Evans, G. W., *A Geographical, Historical, and Topographical Description of Van Diemen's Land*, London 1822.

Gale, W. K. V., *The Iron and Steel Industry: A Dictionary of Terms*, Newton Abbot 1971.

Gillespie, C. C. (ed.), *A Diderot Pictorial Encyclopedia of Trades and Industry* (2 vols), New York 1959.

Glover, M., *History of the Site of Bowen's Settlement, Risdon Cove*, National Parks and Wildlife Service, Tasmania, Occasional Paper 2, Hobart 1978.

Greville's Official Post Office Directory and Gazetteer of New South Wales . . . 1875 to 1877, Sydney n.d.

Greville's Official Post Office Directory of New South Wales, Sydney 1872.

Harcus, W. (ed.), *South Australia and its History, Resources, and Productions*, London 1876.

Harper, L. F. and White, H. P., *Coke*, NSW Department of Mines, Geological Survey, Bulletin 12, Sydney 1924.

Harrod, J. G., *J. G. Harrod's Royal County Directory of Devonshire and Cornwall*, Norwich 1878.

Higginbotham, E. and Jack, R. I, 'The Asgard Swamp Mine and Kiln Near Mt Victoria NSW', *Australian Archaeology*, 15, 1982, 54–66.

Historical Records of New South Wales (7 vols), Sydney 1889–1901.

Hopewell Furnace: A Guide to Hopewell Village National Historic Site, Pennsylvania, National Park Handbook 124, Washington 1983.

Hoskins, C., *The Hoskins Saga*, Sydney 1969.

Hoskins Iron & Steel Co., 'The Black Book', Sydney 1925.

Hoskins Ltd., G. & C., *The Iron Industry and its Development*, 'The Blue Book', Sydney 1915.

Hughes, H., *The Australian Iron and Steel Industry, 1848–1962*, Parkville 1964.

Hume, J. R., *The Industrial Archaeology of Scotland: I, The Lowlands and Borders*, London 1976.

Jack, R. I., 'The Iron and Steel Industry', in Birmingham, J., Jack, I. and Jeans, D., *Australian Pioneer Technology: Sites and Relics*, Richmond Vic. 1979, 87–98.

Jack, R. I., 'William Sandford, a Flawed Ironmaster', *Fourth National Conference on Engineering Heritage 1988*, The Institution of Engineers Australia, 1988, 47–51; also printed in *Transactions of Multi-Disciplinary Engineering* GE, 14, i, 1990, 60–5.

Jaquet, J. B., *The Iron Ore Deposits of New South Wales*, Memoirs of Geological Survey of New South Wales, Geology 2, Sydney 1901.

Jeffries, C. A., 'The Eskbank Iron Works', *The Lone Hand*, 1 June 1911, 183–99.

John, A. H., and Williams, G. (eds), *Glamorgan County History*, V, *Industrial Glamorgan from 1700 to 1900*, Cardiff 1980.

Johnston, R. M., *Systematic Account of the Geology of Tasmania*, Hobart 1888.

Johnston, R. M., *Tasmanian Official Record 1891*, Hobart 1892.

Kenny, J. P. L., 'The Ceramic Kaolin Mine, Lal Lal', *Mining and Geological Journal*, 3, i, March 1947, 22–3.

Krause, F. M., 'The Lal Lal Iron Ore Deposits', *School of Mines, Ballaarat, Annual Report presented at the Meeting of Governors, held February 9th, 1881*, Ballarat 1881, 45–50.

Lewis, E., *Iron and Steel Industry in Australia*, n.p. 1929; also printed in *Selected Papers from the Journal of the Institution of Engineers Australia*, 1, Sydney 1930, 78–113.

Linters, A., *Industria: Industrial Architecture in Belgium*, Liège and Brussels 1986.

Lloyd, J., *The Early History of the Old South Wales Iron Works*, London 1906.

Lockhart, J. R., *The Iron Ore Resources of South Australia*, Geological Survey of South Australia, Bulletin 9, Adelaide 1922.

Lyne, C., *The Industries of New South Wales*, Sydney 1882, 'The Eskbank Iron-works', 107–10.

Lysaght (Aust.) Pty Ltd, J., *Lysaght Venture*, Sydney 1955.

Machattie, T. A., *The Federal Capital: The Case for the West*, Bathurst 1904.

Maddin, R. (ed.), *The Beginning of the Use of Metals and Alloys*, Cambridge Mass. 1988.

Mann, W., *Six Years' Residence in the Australian Colonies Ending in 1839*, London 1839.

McKenzie, E. J., *Thomas Brown, Founder of Lithgow and his Home, Esk Bank*, Katoomba 1969.

Mittagong Iron Week Celebrations Committee, *Centenary of Australia's First Iron Smelting at Mittagong, New South Wales, 1848–1948*, Mittagong 1948.

Mooney, T, *Southern Highlands Discovery*, Bowral 1991.

Morris-Nunn, M., and Tassell, C. B., *Tamar Valley Industrial Heritage: A Survey*, Launceston 1984.

Morrison, W. F., *The Aldine Centennial History of New South Wales*, Sydney 1888.

Muhly, J. D., 'The Beginnings of Metallurgy in the Old World' in R. Maddin (ed.), *The Beginning of the Use of Metals and Alloys*, Cambridge Mass. 1988, 2–20.

Murray, R. and White, K., *The Ironworkers: A History of the Federated Ironworkers' Association of Australia*, Sydney 1982.

Needham, G. R., and Thomson, D. I., *Men of Metal: A Chronicle of the Metal-Casting Industry in South Australia, 1836–1986*, Adelaide 1987.

NSW Department of Mines, *Annual Reports*, Sydney 1875–1930.

NSW Legislative Assembly: Parliamentary Papers, 1911, 2nd Session, 'Report of Royal Commission on the Iron and Steel Industry'.

NSW Legislative Assembly: Parliamentary Papers, 1923, 'Parliamentary Standing Committee on Public Works, Report together with Minutes of Evidence, Appendices and Plan relating to the proposed railway from Moss Vale to Port Kembla'.

NSW Legislative Assembly: Votes and Proceedings, 1907, 2nd Session, 'Development of Iron and Steel Industry'.

NSW Legislative Council: Votes and Proceedings, 1853, I, 807–9, 'Coal at the Fitz Roy Mines'.

'New South Wales Mines and Mineral Statistics', *New South Wales Intercolonial and Philadelphia International Exhibition*, Sydney 1875, 240–1.

Overman, F., *The Manufacture of Iron in all its Various Branches*, 3rd edn, Philadelphia 1854.

Queen Victoria Museum and Art Gallery, *Launceston: A Pictorial History*, Launceston 1989.

Raymond, R., *Out of the Fiery Furnace: The Impact of Metals on the History of Mankind*, South Melbourne 1984.

Read, J., *Explosives*, Harmondsworth 1942.

Rees, D. M., *The Industrial Archaeology of Wales*, Newton Abbot 1975.

Rees, D. M., *Mines, Mills and Furnaces: An Introduction to Industrial Archaeology in Wales*, London 1969.

Robertson, E. G. and Robertson, J., *Cast Iron Decoration: A World Survey*, London 1977.

Russell, P. H., 'Sir Peter Nicol Russell, 1816–1905: His Family and Associates, Pioneers of the Australian Iron and Engineering Industry', *Journal of Royal Australian Historical Society*, 50, 1964, 129–43.

Should Lithgow Be the State Workshop?, Lithgow 1914.

Smith, C., *Town with a History: Beaconsfield Tasmania*, rev. edn, Beaconsfield 1985.

Smith, S. D., Stripling C. P. and Brannon, J. M., *A Cultural Resource Survey of Tennessee's Western Highland Rim Iron Industry, 1790s–1930s*, Tennessee Department of Conservation, Division of Archaeology, Research Series 8, Nashville 1988.

South Australian Department of Mines, 'Mount Jagged Iron Mine', *Mining Review*, 23, 1915, 39–41.

Southern, J. L. N. and Platt, J. E. A., *The History of Ironmaking in Australia, 1848–1914*, Australian Pig Iron Club 1, Port Kembla 1986.

Thomas, D. E. and Baragwanath, W., 'Geology of the Brown Coals of Victoria', *Mining and Geological Journal*, 4, ii, September 1950, 41–63.

Twelvetrees, W. H. and Reid, A. McI., *The Iron Ore Deposits of Tasmania,* Tasmania Department of Mines, Geological Survey, Mineral Resources 6, Hobart 1919.

Ure, A., *A Dictionary of Arts, Manufactures and Mines: Containing a Clear Exposition of their Principles and Practice*, 4th edn (2 vols), London 1853; 5th edn (3 vols), London 1860.

'A Visit to the Lignite Deposits at Lal Lal, near Ballaarat', *Dicker's Mining Record*, 3, June 1864, 100–1.

Wellington, H., *The Ilfracombe Blast Furnace 1872: An Historical and Technical Study of One of Australia's Earliest Iron Smelters*, Grubb Shaft Museum, For the Enthusiast 1, Beaconsfield 1992.

White, W., *History, Gazetteer and Directory of Devonshire*, Sheffield 1850.

White, W., *History, Gazetteer and Directory of Devonshire*, Sheffield 1878–9.

Whitmore, R. L., *Coke Oven Technology in the Ipswich Area*, Department of Mining and Metallurgical Engineering, University of Queensland, 1983.

Williams, J. M., *A Guide to Iron and Steel Pictures in the Hagley Museum and Library*, Wilmington 1986.

Wills, N. R., *Economic Development of the Australian Iron and Steel Industry*, Sydney 1948.

Wright, C. R. A., 'Iron', *Encyclopaedia Britannica*, 9th edn, Edinburgh 1880, XIII, 278–359.

Wylie, R. F. and Singleton, C. C., 'The Railway Crossing of the Blue Mountains, 7, Lithgow', *Australian Railway Historical Society Bulletin*, new series 10, no. 257, March 1959.

Unpublished Reports and Papers

Cash, D., 'A Dream Unfulfilled: The Rise and Fall of Iron Smelting in Tasmania, 1872–1878', unpublished paper to ANZAAS, 1982.

Cremin, A. and Jack, I., 'Lithgow Blast Furnace Site: Archaeological Survey', unpub. report to Council of the City of Greater Lithgow and NSW Department of Planning, 1986.

Downey, R. W., 'Lithgow as an Industrial Centre: History of Industry in Lithgow, 1870–1912', University of Sydney, BA Hons thesis, 1972.

Dunn, E. J., 'Notes on Fireclay and Iron Ore Deposits at Lal Lal', unpublished report to Geological Survey of Victoria, 4 July 1910, Department of Manufacturing and Industry Development (Victoria) Library, report 1910/995, 1.

Hewitt, A. M. et al.,'General Notes on Important Iron Ore Deposits in the State of Victoria', unpub. report to Geological Survey of Victoria, 21 November 1910. Department of Manufacturing and Industry Development (Victoria) Library, report 1910/1756, 7–8; includes transcript of Krause, F. M., 'Lal Lal', 17 August 1877.

'Ilfracombe Iron Company', n.d., 6pp. typescript at Grubb Shaft Museum, Beaconsfield.

McInnes, R. J., 'Lithgow, 1869–1930: An Outline Economic History of the Town', University of NSW, B. Comm. thesis, 1972.

Reynolds, D. K. 'The Ilfracombe Iron Company, Beaconsfield, Tasmania: A Report of Site Inspections and the Interpretations of the Observations of the Evidence Found from these Inspections, Made during February and March 1992', Wollongong, June 1992.

Staughton, P. S. and Ashley, R. W. P., 'The Lal Lal Blast Furnace Reserve Report', n.p. 1976, copy in La Trobe Library, State Library of Victoria.

Thams, P., 'Fitzroy Iron Works: History and Archaeological Survey', Historical Archaeology, University of Sydney 1991.

Wellington, H. K., 'Further Background to the Museum Model and Comments on Reports by Reynolds and Wellington', Launceston, September 1992.

White, W., *History, Gazetteer and Directory of Devonshire*, Sheffield 1850, 752.

Newspapers

Australasian Sketcher, 8 July 1876; 10 May 1879.
Bathurst Daily Times, 1882–6; 1891.
Border Post (Albury), 1874.
Bunyip, 9 November 1872.
Cornwall Chronicle, 1873–4.
Courier (Ballarat), 11 May 1968.
English Mechanic and World of Science, 16 January 1874.
Evening News, 30 March 1895.
Goulburn Herald, 2 September 1876.
Illustrated Adelaide News, January 1875.
Illustrated Australian News, 29 December 1875; 12 June, 10 July, 4 October, 29 November, 27 December 1876; 28 November 1878.
Illustrated Sydney News, 15 April 1869; 27 September 1873; 12 November 1875; 22 July 1876.
Launceston Examiner, 1873–4.
Lithgow Mercury, 1899–1920.
National Advocate, 16 January 1894; 2 December 1911.
Sydney Morning Herald, March 1865; July–September 1868.
Yass Courier, 1873–4.

Manuscripts, photographs and artefacts

Beaconsfield, Grubb Shaft Museum, artefacts from Tasmanian ironworks.
Blue Mountains Lake, NY, The Adirondack Museum, photographs of Standish Blast Furnace, P47858–61.
Canberra, National Library of Australia, pictorial section.
Launceston, Queen Victoria Museum and Art Gallery, mould for plaque to celebrate first smelting at Ilfracombe 1873.
Launceston, Queen Victoria Museum and Art Gallery, photographic collection.
Launceston, State Library of Tasmania, Local Studies Collection, Webb collection of photographs Ilfracombe 1975.
Lithgow, Eskbank House museum, photographic collection.
Lithgow City Library, photographic collection; unpublished reports.
Melbourne, Department of Manufacturing and Industry Development, Minerals Group, Library, photographic collection; unpublished reports.
Melbourne, La Trobe Library, State Library of Victoria, photographic collection.
Mittagong Public School, two lions cast from Fitzroy iron in 1850.
Port Kembla, BHP Archive, Lithgow engineering drawings.

Private ownership, Minute-book of Fitzroy Ironworks Company 1864–72.

Sydney, New South Wales State Library, Mitchell Library, Norton Smith papers (ML A 5317–2/111); Sandford papers (ML MSS 1556); Hoskins papers (ML MSS 4361); pictorial collections.

Sydney, New South Wales State Rail Archives, spade and wheelbarrow made from Fitzroy iron in 1850.

Sydney, Powerhouse Museum, photographic collection, album containing views of Eskbank Ironworks in 1870s.

Sydney, University of Sydney, Macleay Museum, Historic Photographs Collection, photographs of Lithgow.

INDEX